AQA English Literature A: Victorian Literature

AS

Exclusively endorsed by AQA

Ian Stewart

Nelson Thornes

Published in 2008 by:
Nelson Thornes Ltd
Delta Place
27 Bath Road
CHELTENHAM
GL53 7TH
United Kingdom

08 09 10 11 12 / 10 9 8 7 6 5 4 3 2 1

A catalogue record for this book is available from the British Library

ISBN 978 0 7487 8293 1

Cover photographs by Photolibrary and Alamy

Page make-up by Pantek Arts Ltd, Maidstone, Kent

Printed and bound in Croatia by Zrinski

Acknowledgements
Every effort has been made to contact copyright holders and we apologise if any have been inadvertently overlooked. The publisher will be happy to make any necessary amendments at reprint.

The authors and publisher would like to thank the following for permission to reproduce photographs and other copyright material:

p. 8 *Work* by Ford Madox Brown/© Manchester City Galleries; p.13 ©Tate, London, 2008; p. 30 *The Last of England* by Ford Madox Brown/© Birmingham Museums and Art Gallery; p. 35 and 36 © Tate, London, 2008; p. 37 The Blessed Damozel, 1875–79 (oil on canvas) by Rossetti, Dante Charles Gabriel (1828–82) © Lady Lever Art Gallery, National Museums Liverpool/The Bridgeman Art Library; p. 42 © Tate, London, 2008; p. 44 © (a) Science Museum/Science & Society Picture Library; p. 44 (b) © Tate, London, 2008; p. 48 © Blake of Longton, Potteries Museum & Art Gallery, Henley, Stoke-on-Trent; p. 50 © Tate, London, 2008; p. 52 © The Print Collector/Alamy; p. 55 © Mary Evans Picture Library; p. 58 © Reproduced by permission of the Record Office for Leicestershire, Leicester and Rutland; p. 62 © Mary Evans Picture Library/Alamy; p. 64 The Garden of Eden, 1901 (oil on canvas) by Riviere, Hugh Goldwin (1869–1956) © Guildhall Art Gallery, City of London/The Bridgeman Art Gallery; p. 69 © Tate, London, 2008; p. 73 In The Birch Tree Forest, 1883 (oil on canvas) by Shishkin, Ivan Ivanovich (1832–98) © State Russian Museum, St. Petersburg, Russia/The Bridgeman Art Library; p. 75 © Content Mine International/Alamy; p. 81 Joseph Mallord William Turner, Rain, Steam, and Speed – The Great Western Railway, Turner Bequest, 1856, © National Gallery, London; p. 82 © National Portrait Gallery, London; p. 84 © National Portrait Gallery, London; p. 85 The Dinner Hour, Wigan, 1874 (oil on canvas) by Crowe, Eyre (1824–1910) © Manchester Art Gallery, UK/The Bridgeman Art Library; p. 87 Nocturne in Black and Gold, the Falling Rocket, c.1875 (oil on panel) by Whistler, James Abbott McNeill (1834–1903) © The Detroit Institute of Arts, USA/Gift of Dexter M. Ferry Jr./The Bridgeman Art Library; p. 91 © NRM/Science & Society Picture Library

Contents

AQA introduction

Nelson Thornes and AQA

Nelson Thornes has worked in collaboration with AQA to ensure that this book offers you the best support for your AS or A Level course and helps you to prepare for your exams. The partnership means that you can be confident that the range of learning, teaching and assessment practice materials has been checked by the senior examining team at AQA before formal approval, and is closely matched to the requirements of your specification.

Blended learning

Printed and electronic resources are blended: this means that links between topics and activities between the book and the electronic resources help you to work in the way that best suits you, and enable extra support to be provided online. For example, you can test yourself online and feedback from the test will direct you back to the relevant parts of the book.

Electronic resources are available in a simple-to-use online platform called Nelson Thornes learning space. If your school or college has a licence to use the service, you will be given a password through which you can access the materials through any internet connection.

Icons in this book indicate where there is material online related to that topic. The following icons are used:

Learning activity

These resources include a variety of interactive and non-interactive activities to support your learning.

Progress tracking

These resources include a variety of tests that you can use to check your knowledge on particular topics (Test yourself) and a range of resources that enable you to analyse and understand examination questions (On your marks...).

Research support

These resources include WebQuests, in which you are assigned a task and provided with a range of web links to use as source material for research.

Study skills

These resources support you as you develop a skill that is key for your course, for example planning essays.

Analysis tool

These resources help you to analyse key texts and images by providing questions and prompts to focus your response.

When you see an icon, go to Nelson Thornes learning space at **www.nelsonthornes.com/aqagce**, enter your access details and select your course. The materials are arranged in the same order as the topics in the book, so you can easily find the resources you need.

How to use this book

This book covers the specification for your course and is arranged in a sequence approved by AQA. The book is divided into eight chapters, beginning, in Chapter 1 with an introduction to the English Literature A Specification and how you will be assessed. Chapters 2 and 3 explain your exam and coursework tasks and texts. Chapters 4 to 6 each provide guidance on your wider reading in the genres of poetry, prose and drama. Chapter 7 helps to familiarise you with the context question, exploring examples of the type of extracts you might be expected to deal with in the examination. Finally, Chapter 8 takes you through an examination paper, demonstrating how to tackle the paper and focus your answer using keywords.

Aims of the chapter

At the beginning of each section you will find a list of learning objectives that contain targets linked to the requirements of the specification.

The features in this book include:

Key terms

Terms that you will need to be able to define and understand. These terms are coloured blue in the textbook and their definition will also appear in the glossary at the back of this book.

Did you know?

Interesting facts to extend your background knowledge.

Links

Links to refer you to other areas of the book which cover the topics you are reading about.

Further reading

Suggestions for other texts that will help you in your study and preparation for assessment in English literature.

Activity

Activities which develop the skills you will need for success in your English literature course.

Questions

Questions which help to focus your reading of key extracts and prepare you for writing on extracts in the exam and in your coursework.

AQA Examination-style questions

Questions in the style that you can expect in your exam. You will find these in Chapter 8.

Summary

A summary of what is covered in each chapter of the book.

AQA examination questions are reproduced by permission of the Assessment and Qualifications Alliance.

1 Introduction

Aims of the chapter:

- ▪ Introduces the content and skills requirements of the AS course.

- ▪ Considers the philosophy of reading and meaning that underpins the Specification.

- ▪ Explores the choices you can make in your wider reading.

- ▪ Explains how you will be assessed.

This book has been written to help you to be as successful as possible in your AS AQA English Literature A course. It will introduce you to the relevant **subject matter** that you need to **know and understand**, as well as to the **skills** you need to develop and apply in order to read, analyse, interpret and write about your texts.

In this chapter we look at:

- ▪ the kinds of reading you will be undertaking
- ▪ the wider reading list
- ▪ the Assessment Objectives
- ▪ the marking grid.

This book will give you help, support and advice on:

- ▪ how to approach your set texts
- ▪ how to succeed with your coursework
- ▪ how to tackle wider reading in prose, poetry and drama
- ▪ approaches to wide reading in non-fiction
- ▪ a sample exam paper.

▪ Your AS English Literature course

This is one of three AS textbooks for AQA English Literature Specification A – one each for the three optional areas of study. Your chosen option is Victorian Literature, which is the focus for this book and all your reading for the AS course. You will be studying **one poetry** text for the written exam, and **one prose** text and **one drama** text for your coursework.

You will also need to read widely in Victorian literature. Your wider reading will probably include some whole texts, but will no doubt also include a good many extracts. Reading the extracts will help you to appreciate the variety and range of Victorian literature, covering writers of both **genders** as well as texts of all **genres**.

Your teacher will establish the foundation and framework for your reading, but as you progress through your AS course, and once you gain confidence and experience as a reader, **you** should increasingly be the one who chooses and explores aspects of the literature. You will then be in a position to be able to pursue your own interests, tracing connections, comparisons and contrasts between texts in the **shared context** of Victorian literature. Your study of the chosen area of literature will therefore consist of both **close and wide reading**.

How to become an informed, independent reader

Before we start to explore your chosen area of literature, we are going to establish what kind of reader you need to be. The aim of AS English Literature is to enable you to develop as an informed, independent reader and confident critic of literary texts.

As an informed, independent reader, you will learn to build a reading of a text through:

■ careful and close reading which provides you with appropriate and specific evidence to support your interpretation

■ consideration and understanding of other possible readings

■ research into the contexts of both reading and writing.

The AQA English Literature A Specification provides you, the reader, with maximum opportunities for both writing coursework and for sitting an open-text exam (an exam where you are allowed to take a copy of your set text into the exam and are encouraged to use it to help answer the questions). Such opportunities encourage research on the one hand, and close focus on specific parts of texts on the other.

Reading for meaning

As you read the literature of your chosen period, you will need to be actively engaged with your texts in order to develop informed, personal responses.

The AQA English Literature course is built on a philosophy of reading and meaning which it is important that you understand and share.

We think that:

Reading:

■ is an active process: the reader is an **active creator**, not a passive recipient of second-hand opinion – *you are the 'maker of meaning'*

■ can never be 'innocent': all readings are historically, socially and individually specific – *you bring your own personal context and experience to the text*

■ is not a single skill: some kinds of reading are more demanding than others – *think, for example, of the comparable difficulty of reading a Mills and Boon romance on the one hand, and a Jane Austen novel on the other.*

Meaning:

■ for an individual reader, depends as much on what is brought to the text as on what is contained within it – *your own experience will influence the way you read the text*

■ will not necessarily be instantly accessible – *you may well need to research **difficult or obscure** references and vocabulary, for example, before you can tease out meaning*

■ will be different on different occasions, and changeable as a result of discussion and reflection – *when you reread a text, for example, you may find your response is different from your first reading; discussion with your peers or your teacher, or reading a critical commentary, may also influence and change your response to a text*

■ can be multiple; different readings of a text can coexist – *you need to be aware that some texts are ambiguous or capable of delivering multiple meanings, and it is your own selection of and response to textual evidence that will determine your **own personal** interpretation.*

Wider reading for your AS English Literature course

Your AS course, then, is a coherent collection of reading in Victorian literature. The texts for detailed study (the set poetry text in the exam and the novel and play in your coursework) are supported by your wider reading, which provides the context.

The purpose of your wider reading is to:

- provide you with the opportunity to discover and explore your own interests and enjoyment, developing your awareness of the ways you respond to and understand different kinds of writing
- enable you to consider the **typicality** or **shared context** of your reading so that you can explore connections, comparisons and contrasts
- encourage you to see different points of view, exploring the ways that different writers describe a similar experience or situation
- enable you to discover and understand the ways different writers choose to communicate with you, the reader, exploring choices of form, structure and language.

The Specification for the AQA AS English Literature A course provides you with a reading list from which you and your teachers can choose whole texts and extracts for study. It covers all relevant **genres**, writing by both **male and female authors**, significant and influential **literature in translation**, as well as **non-fiction texts**. The wider reading list is set out below.

Texts for AS – Victorian Literature

(* denotes post-1990)

Choose three texts (or the equivalent in extracts) of any genre.

Prose fiction

Peter Ackroyd, *The Last Testament of Oscar Wilde* (1983)

*Beryl Bainbridge, *Master Georgie* (1998)

Arnold Bennett, *Anna of the Five Towns* (1902)

*Andrew Drummond, *An Abridged History* (2004)

Elizabeth Gaskell, *Mary Barton* (1848)

G. & W. Grossmith, *The Diary of a Nobody* (1892)

*Andrew Martin, *The Necropolis Railway* (2002)

Herman Melville, *Redburn* (1849)

William Morris, *News from Nowhere* (1891)

Robert Louis Stevenson, *The Strange Case of Dr Jekyll and Mr Hyde* (1886)

Prose non-fiction

Victorian non-fiction

Matthew Arnold, *Culture and Anarchy* (1869)

Thomas Carlyle, *Selected Writings* (Penguin)

John Clare, *Selected Letters* (OUP)

Elizabeth Gaskell, *The Life of Charlotte Brontë* (1857)

Edmund Gosse, *Father and Son* (1907)

Marx and Engels, *The Communist Manifesto* (1848)

John Ruskin, *Selected Writings* (Penguin)

The Brontës (ed. Barker), *A Life in Letters*

Henry Thoreau, *Walden* (1854)

Oscar Wilde, *De Profundis* (1905)

Modern non-fiction

*Peter Ackroyd, *Dickens* (1990)

*Juliet Barker, *The Brontës* (1994)

*Jonathan Bate, *John Clare* (2003)

Quentin Bell, *A New and Noble School* (1982)

*Barbara Dennis, *The Victorian Novel* (2000)

*Terry Eagleton, *Heathcliff and the Great Hunger* (1996)

Richard Ellman, *Oscar Wilde* (1988)

*Alice Jenkins and Juliet John, *Re-reading Victorian Fiction* (2002)

Lytton Strachey, *Eminent Victorians* (1918)

*Claire Tomalin, *Thomas Hardy: The Time-Torn Man* (2006)

Drama

Anonymous, *Maria Marten, or Murder in the Red Barn* (1840)

J.M. Barrie, *The Admirable Crichton* (1902)

Dion Boucicault, *The Streets of London* (1864)

Terry Eagleton, *Saint Oscar* (1989)

*Brian Friel, *The Home Place* (2005)

Patrick Hamilton, *Gaslight* (1939)

*David Hare, *The Judas Kiss* (1998)

Arthur Wing Pinero, *The Second Mrs Tanqueray* (1893)

Harold Pinter, *The French Lieutenant's Woman* (screenplay) (1981)

George Bernard Shaw, *Mrs Warren's Profession* (1894)

George Bernard Shaw, *Arms and the Man* (1898)

*Tom Stoppard, *The Invention of Love* (1997)

Tom Taylor, *The Ticket-of-Leave Man* (1863)

Oscar Wilde, *Lady Windermere's Fan* (1892)

Oscar Wilde, *An Ideal Husband* (1895)

Oscar Wilde, *The Importance of Being Earnest* (1895)

Poetry

Matthew Arnold

Elizabeth Barrett Browning

Robert Browning

Arthur Clough

Emily Dickinson

Gerald Manley Hopkins

A.E. Housman

George Meredith

Christina Rossetti

Algernon Swinburne

Alfred, Lord Tennyson

Walt Whitman

Texts in translation

Anton Chekhov, *Uncle Vanya* (1897)

Feodor Dostoevsky, *Crime and Punishment* (1866)

Gustave Flaubert, *Madame Bovary* (1857)

Gustave Flaubert, *Sentimental Education* (1869)

Nikolai Gogol, *The Government Inspector* (1836)

Henrik Ibsen, *An Enemy of the People* (1882)

August Strindberg, *Miss Julie* (1888)

Leo Tolstoy, *Anna Karenin* (1875)

Emile Zola, *Germinal* (1885)

Emile Zola, *La Bête humaine* (1890)

Keeping a record of your reading will be very important, especially as you will be dealing with a good many extracts. We suggest that you keep a detailed **Reading Log**; at the end of the course this will provide a very useful revision tool. Another useful thing to do would be to place all your reading in the shared context on a **timeline**.

Close reading for your AS English Literature course

Not only is it important that you read widely throughout the course, but you must also ensure that you develop the skills of **close reading**. You will need these skills in every answer you write and they underpin the whole of your AS English Literature course.

Close reading of a text will enable you to **analyse** and **explore** a writer's techniques – his or her choices of form, structure and language – and will help you to:

- respond fully to meaning or possible meanings of the text
- gain understanding of the ways texts work
- find textual evidence to support your interpretation.

If you are the kind of reader who does **not** read closely, you will only be able to offer a **skimpy** reading of your texts, based on **unsupported assertion**. This will not be sufficient for you to be successful in your AS English Literature course. Nor is there any point in counting numbers of syllables, making exaggerated claims for alliteration, or setting out a pattern of rhyme (ababcc, for example), unless this research is part of an analysis or exploration of the ways the writer's choices make meaning for you.

It is important that you adopt good reading habits:

- You should read every whole text or extract three or four times in order to mine it thoroughly; the first reading will be for general impression, the subsequent ones will enable you to explore the writer's techniques fully.
- Initially you will respond to subject matter and theme.
- Then you need to move on to the ways the writer expresses the subject matter.

In order to analyse the ways writers write, you need to ask yourself particular questions:

- What kind of text is this?
- When was this text written?
- What is the subject matter?
- Who is speaking and how does the writer use the idea of 'voice' in the text?
- How does the writer use setting(s)?
- How does the writer use ideas of time? (past, present, future)
- How does the writer structure, organise and develop the ideas in the text?
- Is there anything distinctive in the way the text is written? (structure, choices of vocabulary, sentence structures, variations in pace ...)
- Are there any patterns, repetitions of key ideas or images, or uses of contrast?
- What kinds of language are used? (formal, informal, descriptive, dialogue, and so on)
- How has finding out more about the references and allusions in the text added to my understanding and interpretation?

■ Is the language all the same or does the writer use contrast?

■ What is the tone of the text?

■ What might be the writer's purpose in this text?

All the answers to these questions need to be related to your own interpretation of the text, and to your own making of meaning.

How your work will be assessed

Your wider reading in the poetry, prose and drama of Victorian literature, as well as your knowledge and understanding of your chosen poetry text, will be assessed in Unit 1. You will write two essays in a two-hour exam. This unit carries 60% of AS or 30% of A2 marks. In Unit 2 (coursework) you will write two more essays, one on your prose text and one on your drama text. The folder as a whole will be about 2,500 words in length and carries 40% of AS or 20% of A2 marks.

All your work for the course will be assessed against four Assessment Objectives (AOs):

AO1 Articulate creative, informed and relevant responses to literary texts, using appropriate terminology and concepts, and coherent, accurate written expression (*your ability to use your knowledge and understanding, to focus on the task, and to express yourself appropriately*).

AO2 Demonstrate detailed critical understanding in analysing the ways in which structure, form and language shape meanings in literary texts (*your ability to explore the ways the writers' choices of form, structure and language influence the ways you interpret texts and make meaning*).

AO3 Explore connections and comparisons between different literary texts, informed by interpretations of other readers (*your ability to find links between the texts you read and to explore alternative readings*).

AO4 Demonstrate understanding of the significance and influence of the contexts in which literary texts are written and received (*your ability to assess where and how your texts fit into the shared context*).

These four Assessment Objectives are used to measure your achievement throughout the Specification and are organised by your examiners into a marking grid, which is used to assess each piece of work that you do throughout your course. You, and your teachers, will be able to check your performance against the criteria in the grid. Each of the AOs is divided into 'bands' (see the table opposite).

If your work has the features of **Band 1** work – inaccurate, irrelevant, assertive – you will not be writing at the required standard for AS.

If your work is assessed as falling into **Band 2**, it is judged to be narrative and descriptive and rather generalised in its approach to texts.

If your work is assessed as falling within **Band 3**, it means that you are starting to explore and analyse the texts and presenting your work in a coherent fashion.

If your work is assessed as falling into **Band 4,** it is coherent, cogent, mature and sophisticated, and worthy of the highest grade.

Marking grid for Units 1 and 2

	Assessment Objectives			
	AO1	AO2	AO3	AO4
	AO1: Articulate creative, informed and relevant responses to literary texts, using appropriate terminology and concepts, and coherent, accurate written expression	AO2: Demonstrate detailed critical understanding in analysing the ways in which structure, form and language shape meanings in literary texts	AO3: Explore connections and comparisons between different literary texts, informed by interpretations of other readers	AO4: Demonstrate understanding of the significance and influence of the contexts in which literary texts are written and received
Band 1	Candidates characteristically: ■ communicate limited knowledge and understanding of literary texts ■ make few uses of appropriate terminology or examples to support interpretations ■ attempt to communicate meaning by using inaccurate language.	Candidates characteristically: ■ identify few aspects of structure, form and language ■ assert some aspects with reference to how they shape meaning.	Candidates characteristically: ■ make few links between literary texts ■ reflect the views expressed in other interpretations of literary texts in a limited way.	Candidates characteristically: ■ communicate limited understanding of context through descriptions of culture, text type, literary genre or historical period.
Band 2	Candidates characteristically: ■ communicate some basic knowledge and understanding of literary texts ■ make simple use of appropriate terminology or examples to support interpretations ■ communicate meaning using straightforward language.	Candidates characteristically: ■ identify obvious aspects of structure, form and language ■ describe some aspects with reference to how they shape meaning.	Candidates characteristically: ■ make straightforward links and connections between literary texts ■ reflect the views expressed in other interpretations of literary texts in a basic way.	Candidates characteristically: ■ communicate some basic understanding of context through descriptions of culture, text type, literary genre or historical period.
Band 3	Candidates characteristically: ■ communicate relevant knowledge and understanding of literary texts ■ present relevant responses, using appropriate terminology to support informed interpretations ■ structure and organise their writing ■ communicate content and meaning through expressive and accurate writing.	Candidates characteristically: ■ identify relevant aspects of structure, form and language in literary texts ■ explore how writers use specific aspects to shape meaning ■ use specific references to texts to support their responses.	Candidates characteristically: ■ explore links and connections between literary texts ■ communicate understanding of the views expressed in different interpretations or readings.	Candidates characteristically: ■ communicate understanding of the relationships between literary texts and their contexts ■ comment appropriately on the influence of culture, text type, literary genre or historical period on the ways in which literary texts were written and were – and are – received.
Band 4	Candidates characteristically: ■ communicate relevant knowledge and understanding of literary texts with confidence ■ present relevant, well-informed responses, fluently using appropriate terminology to support informed interpretations ■ structure and organise their writing in a cogent manner ■ communicate content and meaning through sophisticated and mature writing.	Candidates characteristically: ■ identify relevant aspects of structure, form and language in literary texts ■ confidently explore how writers use specific aspects to shape meaning ■ show a mastery of detail in their use of specific texts to support their responses.	Candidates characteristically: ■ explore links and connections between literary texts with confidence ■ communicate understanding of the views expressed in different interpretations or readings in a mature, sophisticated manner.	Candidates characteristically: ■ communicate a mature understanding of the relationships between literary texts and their contexts ■ comment in a sophisticated manner on the influence of culture, text type, literary genre or historical period on the ways in which literary texts were written and were – and are – received.

We now turn to an exploration of the detail of your studies. Each of the sections in this book looks at a different part of your AS English Literature course in more detail:

■ the set texts for Unit 1

■ coursework for Unit 2

■ wider reading in the three genres – poetry, prose and drama

■ how to prepare for the context question in your written exam

■ looking at a sample exam paper and at how to get the best possible marks in your answer.

We begin in the next chapter with a consideration of the set poetry text on the written paper.

Summary

We have now considered:

■ the kinds of reading you will be doing

■ the choices you will be making

■ the skills you need to develop

■ how your work will be assessed.

Fig. 1.1 *'Work' by Ford Madox Brown (1865). This complex allegory of the Victorian social structure depicts a wide variety of workers: to succeed at AS English Literature, you too will have to work in a range of different ways*

Work by Ford Madox Brown, © Manchester City Galleries

How to approach the set text in Unit 1

Aims of the chapter:

■ Introduces the poetry set text, the relevant Assessment Objectives and the types of questions.

■ Considers how you will be assessed in the exam and the best and most effective ways to approach the study of your set text in Unit 1.

Choice of text

There are three poetry texts set for study on this paper; you will study **one** of them. We are going to look at what each text offers in terms of Victorian poetry and at how each editor has approached the task of compiling an anthology.

You will be studying one of the following texts:

Either

1 *The Selected Poems of John Clare* (published 1997)

Although John Clare (1793–1864) is often classified by literary critics as one of the later poets of the Romantic movement, it should be remembered that he was also a Victorian writer. Not only did Clare live through the first 27 years of Victoria's reign, but, in a poem written in the High Beach Asylum around 1840, he exhibited a surprisingly prurient interest in the activities of 'little Vicky' – speculating on which politicians are 'strumming … the queen's snuff-box' when 'Prince Albert goes to Germany'! Unfortunately, this particular poem (a schizophrenic reworking of Byron, entitled *Don Juan: A Poem*) does not feature in your set text – although you can find it in Jonathan Bate's comprehensive 2003 Faber selection.

This Specification's set Clare anthology was selected and arranged by R.K.R. Thornton. The editor has also written an Introduction, as well as providing a Chronology of Clare's life, Notes that include suggestions for wider reading, and a Glossary of the obscure Northamptonshire dialect words that sometimes feature in Clare's poetry. He has chosen 63 poems which span the whole of Clare's poetic output, from his first, best-selling collection, to some of the madhouse poetry which was not published until over a century after Clare's death. Thornton has grouped the poems thematically so that the collection reflects Clare's main concerns as a writer: he explains the reasons for the choices of theme in his Introduction.

The sections into which the editor has arranged his chosen poems are entitled:

A Country Village Year

Birds and Beasts

Love

Loss and the Politics of Nature

John Clare, Poet

The first section's title is obviously meant to echo that of Clare's own third published collection, *The Shepherd's Calendar*, while Thornton admits that the fourth section should probably have been divided into two parts – although the combination does enable him to emphasise the connections between Clare's sense of identity and the Northamptonshire landscape in which he lived.

Or

Link

If you are studying Clare's poetry as your set text, you should pay particular attention to the sample of his prose writing (and the associated further reading suggestions) featured in Chapter 7.

🔃 2 *The Selected Poems of the Brontës* (published 1997)

In contrast to the Specification's two single-poet set anthologies, Pamela Norris's selection features the work of four different writers from the same family. The editor has also written an Introduction and provided illuminating Notes on the background to each poem, along with a Chronology of the Brontës' lives and times. The 74 poems included in this collection are taken from the one volume of the sisters' poetry published during their lifetimes, *Poems by Currer, Ellis and Acton Bell* (1846: it sold only two copies!), and from the imaginary Sagas of Gondal and Angria: the private fantasy worlds created by the Brontës during their childhood. The collection divides the poems into sections by author and the sections are sequenced according to the Brontës' dates of birth; each author's poems are then arranged chronologically within the sections.

The sections into which the editor has arranged her chosen poems along with the number of poems each section contains, are:

Charlotte Brontë (1816–1855) 10 poems

Patrick Branwell Brontë (1817–1848) 15 poems

Emily Jane Brontë (1818–1848) 31 poems

Anne Brontë (1820–1849) 18 poems.

💡 The number of poems in each section may give a slightly misleading impression of the distribution of the editor's choices, as some poems are shorter than others. In fact, Norris devotes about 20 pages to poems by each of Charlotte, Branwell and Anne – with Emily given almost twice as much space. To some extent, the balance of her selection reflects contemporary critical opinion: Emily is acknowledged as the family's finest poet; Charlotte's four novels tend to overshadow her poetry; Anne's writing is 'typically brief and fluent'; while Branwell failed both as a poet and as a painter (and as a private tutor and as a railway booking clerk …).

Or

🔃 3 *The Selected Poems of Thomas Hardy* (published 1998)

Like John Clare, Thomas Hardy (1840–1928) was a writer whose work was not confined to the Victorian era – he lived into the third decade of the 20th century. Unlike Clare, we think of Hardy *primarily* as a Victorian: the novels for which he is best known were all written during the 19th century, while his first collection of poetry, *Wessex Poems*, was published in 1898 and contains poems dating back as far as 1866. Hardy's poetry represents the second phase of his literary career: he produced no new prose fiction after *Jude the Obscure*'s hostile reception in 1895, but went on to publish seven more volumes of poetry after 1898.

💡 Norman Page's anthology comprises 111 of Hardy's poems, written over a period of 62 years. The poems are arranged in a loosely chronological manner and, strictly speaking, not all of them are Victorian. Approximately half of the selected poems were written after 1901, the end of the Victorian era, although Hardy gives some of these later poems specifically Victorian settings by including 19th-century dates in their titles. You do not need to worry about which of the set text's poems were written before 1901 and which were written afterwards: the important things are that you have read the whole collection and that you are familiar with Hardy's poetic techniques. In addition to his selection of poems, the editor has also included a brief Introduction and provided Notes on the background to some of the poems, along with a Chronology of Hardy's life and times.

Link

If you are studying the Brontës' poetry as your set text, you should pay particular attention to the extract from Charlotte Brontë's biography (and the associated further reading suggestions) featured in Chapter 7.

If you are studying Hardy's poetry as your set text, you should try to include at least one of his prose works in your wider reading; you could even write one of your coursework units on a Hardy novel. You will also find that Claire Tomalin's 2006 biography, *Thomas Hardy: The Time-Torn Man*, and Patricia Ingham's 2003 study for Oxford's *Authors in Context* series, provide useful background material.

💡 *To summarise:*

All three texts offer you the chance to study a Victorian poet, but there are key differences between them in terms of the editor's approach:

- Thornton organises his selection of Clare's poems **thematically**, according to his ideas about the principal concerns of Clare's writing.

- Norris arranges the Brontës in chronological order and devotes the most space to Emily because she believes her to be the family's superior poet.

- Page's approach is loosely chronological. He places particular emphasis on Hardy's *Poems of 1912–13*: the poems in which, after his first wife's death, Hardy revisits the scenes of their Victorian courtship.

🔍 💡 Studying the poems in your chosen text

Once your poetry text is chosen, you will need to do all you can to make sure that you are familiar with the whole anthology, and that you understand each poem.

You will need to study each poem individually, as well as the collection as a whole. Here are some suggestions for how you could go about doing this:

1 For each poem:
- Look back to the section on close reading in Chapter 1 and use the prompts and questions to work with each poem.
- Make a note of your responses to the questions, of the ways you interpret each poem, and of how it reflects the Victorian era.
- You should start a Reading Log where you record your responses to each poem. This may be organised in a paper file, or you might like to use the online Reading Log provided for you. You can save this and add to it throughout your course. You can also print it out for revision.

2 For the whole collection:
- Go on to consider how the individual poems connect and compare with each other, in terms of subject matter and style.
- Look at the way the anthology is structured and explore why you think the editor chose to arrange it in this way.
- Try arranging the poems in a different way and assess the changed impact the new structure has on the reader.

The notes you assemble from these activities will help you to produce very useful notes for your revision.

▪ The Assessment Objectives for Unit 1

When you have read and studied your poems closely, you will need to consider the ways in which you will prepare for the exam. Clearly, your preparation needs to be informed by the way in which you will be assessed. We looked at the Assessment Objectives in some detail in Chapter 1, and you may wish to remind yourself of what they are and how they work.

For your set text, there are **three** relevant Assessment Objectives:

AO1 – *your ability to use your knowledge and understanding, to focus on the task, and to express yourself appropriately;*

AO2 – *your ability to explore the ways the writers' choices of form, structure and language influence the ways you interpret texts and make meaning;*

AO3 – *your ability to find links between the poems you study and to explore alternative readings.*

You will be assessed on your ability to meet all three Assessment Objectives, but you will need to remember that the **most important** Assessment Objective is **AO3** – your ability **to connect and compare the poems** as well as **to consider different interpretations**.

⬧ What kinds of questions will you have to answer in the exam?

The three relevant Assessment Objectives are reflected in every question set on your chosen poetry text. You will be given a choice of two questions, and you will answer one of them. All the questions test the same Assessment Objectives.

Each question will set out a view which you are invited to consider. You will need to say how far you agree with the view in the question.

A few examples of the kinds of views that may be expressed in the questions are:

- a named poem as the key to the collection
- a named poem as an appropriate introduction to the collection
- a named poem as an appropriate conclusion to the collection
- a 21st-century reviewer's opinion of the collection
- a modern literary critic's opinion of the poetry
- a 19th-century reader's opinion of the poet.

You can make up your own questions using some or all of these suggestions, swap them with other students and attempt to answer each other's questions. This should help you to develop the receptive, open-minded approach to the ideas of others that is one of the keys to exam success.

Remember that you need to consider the given view, saying how far you agree, through a detailed comparison of several poems from the collection. Most questions invite you to consider two or three poems in some detail, or to range more widely.

■ How will I be assessed in the exam?

Examiners will use the four-band marking grid which we introduced in Chapter 1. They will assess your essay out of 45, using a mark scheme tailored to each question. This mark scheme will relate to:

- the three relevant Assessment Objectives
- the four-band marking grid
- the keywords of the question.

■ Link

Look back to Chapter 1 to see the marking grid examiners will use.

■ Link

If you turn to Chapter 8, you will see sample poetry questions on a specimen paper, as well as a sample mark scheme.

Advice for success:

- Remember that this is still an English Literature exam. Although the questions on your set text will be testing Assessment Objective 3 in particular, meeting Assessment Objectives 1 and 2 is still vital to your success. You will need to be able to write clear, structured answers; you will need to have a secure knowledge of your set text and show that you are able to analyse the writer's use of language and style.

- You will meet the Assessment Objectives if you produce a relevant answer which addresses the keywords of the question you choose: the wording and construction of all the questions are designed to point you towards the appropriate Assessment Objectives.

- Look carefully at the Assessment Grids in Chapter 8: there is a detailed, generic version which applies to all questions, and a question-specific version for each of the questions on your set text. The examiners will be using these grids when they mark your set text answer: the descriptors for each level and Assessment Objective will give you some idea of what they will be looking for.

- You should try to develop the skills necessary for the construction of a balanced argument: these are vital because you will meet Assessment Objective 3 by writing a relevant answer to the question: 'How far do you agree?'

- You should try to think for yourself when responding to your chosen set text question. Although it is not compulsory, you may refer to any critics you have read if you wish to. However, **your own ideas** are the most important: the question will invite you to express your answer in the first person.

- Remember, as this is an open-book exam, there will usually be a question that requires you to focus on a specific poem or group of poems.

- It is important that you back up your ideas by close reference to the poetry when answering your set text question, but keep the quotations short: examiners know that a candidate who copies out large chunks of the text is probably struggling to cope.

- Remember that you are expected to be familiar with the whole of the poetry collection you have studied.

- Make the effort to read around the set text you are studying. Wider reading can provide important background information on your set poet within the Victorian context, as well as giving you the chance to consider other perspectives on the poetry which will help you to address Assessment Objective 3.

What to avoid:

- Do not respond to the exam question by writing an account of the poet's life and times. A successful answer to the question might include some relevant biographical information, but it is important that you display your contextual knowledge *through* your knowledge of the poetry.

- Do not write an answer that wholly agrees (or disagrees) with the view that is set up for discussion in the question: such a one-sided, unbalanced response will be given a Band 2 mark, no matter how good your textual knowledge is, because you will not have met Assessment Objective 3.

- Do not abuse the open-book exam by copying anything out of the introduction or the notes included in your set text. The examiners will spot what you have done and they know that anyone who tries it must be desperate: unassimilated critical material is often a feature of Band 1 answers.

- Do not recycle your practice answers when you sit the exam. The questions are never the same as those set previously, so twisting an earlier essay in an attempt to fit it to a new question usually ends in disaster. You must approach each question afresh.

Fig. 2.1 *Victorian values: the homeless queue for overnight shelter in 'Applicants for Admission to a Casual Ward' by Sir Luke Fildes (1874). One of the posters on the wall reads 'Child Deserted: £2 Reward', another announces 'Lost, a pug dog: £20 Reward'*

3　Approaching the coursework

Introduction

For Unit 2 you will be asked to present a folder of coursework that contains two pieces of writing: one will be an essay on a prose text, the other on a drama text. Both texts will come from the shared context of Victorian literature. You will be given a list of 10 prose texts and a list of three drama texts from which you can make your choices. When you have studied your two chosen texts, you will then negotiate the two tasks with your teacher. Your teacher will make sure that both of your agreed tasks reflect the relevant Assessment Objectives.

A moderator, the representative of the Examination Board, will be assigned to approve the tasks that you have agreed with your teacher or to give advice when any changes need to be made to the tasks you have chosen. The total number of words that you will be asked to write for the two tasks together is between 2,000 and 2,500 words.

In this chapter we:

■ explore the opportunities offered by coursework for you to work in different ways

■ look at each of the 10 prose texts (from which you will have to choose the two you want to study and write about in your coursework)

■ explore the kinds of tasks that are appropriate in order to reflect the relevant Assessment Objectives

■ look at the three drama texts (from which you will have to choose the one you want to study and write about in your coursework)

■ explore the kinds of coursework tasks that are appropriate in order to reflect the Assessment Objectives.

Coursework – a different way of working

Your coursework will give you opportunities to work in ways that are very different from the way you would prepare for an exam. You will need to make the most of these opportunities in order to gain the maximum marks for your coursework. You will plan and write your coursework by working through the following stages, each of which gives you the opportunity to make the most of your work.

1 Negotiating the task
Once you have chosen your two coursework texts, and you have read and studied them in detail, you will have time to think about **what particularly interests you** about the texts. Finding an appropriate **focus** for your writing is a crucial first step. Having taken it, you can then start to consider the kind of task you will negotiate with your teacher. Unlike the exam in Unit 1 where an examiner writes the questions, in the coursework you and your teacher are responsible for deciding the task. Of course, it must be constructed within the guidelines laid down by the Board, and we will look at those guidelines towards the end of the chapter.

2 Research
Once you have agreed your task with your teacher and it has been approved by the exam board moderator, you will have the time and

opportunity to carry out your own **research** on the topic you have chosen. You will need to organise yourself well and decide how you will keep the notes you take down in a systematic way so that they are of most use to you. You will, of course, need to keep a note of any sources that you consult, other than the primary text, as you will be expected to acknowledge these at the end of your essay.

3   Writing
When you are confident that you have done all the necessary reading and research, and have all the information that you require, you can turn to the actual writing of your essay. One advantage of writing coursework is that you can consult your teacher at any stage of the process. You will need to:

- plan carefully
- select the relevant material
- organise and structure your writing
- write the first **draft**.

You may wish to use the online planning tool to support planning your coursework.

You can, of course, show this draft to your teacher for comment, and you can then **redraft** your essay in the light of any advice or suggestions they give you.

4   Ensuring the quality of written communication and presentation
Your coursework gives you the opportunity to reconsider, to rethink your ideas, and then to draft and redraft your work. You will therefore be expected to present work that is well written, accurate and fluent, and well presented. If you choose to write your essays by hand, then it is important that your writing is legible. If you choose to word-process your work (as most candidates do), then it is important that you consider presentation and appearance. You should use a standard font that is clear and easy to read. You should use a font size no smaller than 12 points, and you should not type your entire essay in italics or capitals.

The prose text

We are now going to look at each of the 10 prose texts from which you will be choosing one to study and write about in your coursework. The texts cover the period 1847 to 2000; four are by female and six by male authors. You will choose **one** of these texts and write a coursework essay on it.

We will consider the texts **chronologically**, in the order in which they were written.

1 *Jane Eyre* by Charlotte Brontë (1816–1855)

This novel was published in 1847.

Biography

Charlotte Brontë was the oldest surviving child of the Reverend Patrick Brontë of Haworth: her two elder sisters, Maria and Elizabeth, died as a result of the harsh conditions at the boarding school attended by four of the Brontë children. From the age of 18, Charlotte worked sporadically as a teacher and a governess in Yorkshire and in Brussels, often spending the time between jobs nursing members of her family through their illnesses. Although Charlotte Brontë's first novel, *The Professor*, did not appear in print until after her death, her first published novel, *Jane Eyre* (released under the pseudonym Currer Bell), was an immediate success. Her subsequent novels *Shirley* (1849) and *Villette* (1854) were also popular with Victorian readers. In 1854, despite strong opposition from her father, she married his curate, the Reverend Arthur Nicholls. Unfortunately, Charlotte Brontë died several months later, her fatal illness caused by complications in the early stages of pregnancy, and by exhaustion from the years devoted to caring for her ailing family.

Story

Jane Eyre lives at Gateshead Hall with her aunt Mrs Reed, who, after Jane's outspoken responses to the bullying she receives from her cousins, consigns her to Lowood, an institution for orphans which closely resembles the school attended by the Brontë sisters. Despite her early unhappiness at the school, Jane grows up to become a teacher there. Eventually Jane moves to a post as governess at Thornfield Hall, where she falls in love with her employer, Mr Rochester. She agrees to marry him, but their wedding is dramatically interrupted by Rochester's brother-in-law, who reveals that Rochester is already married: his wife is now mad and is kept locked in an attic at Thornfield. Jane flees across the moors and is taken in by the Rivers family of Marsh End, who turn out to be her long-lost cousins. Jane discovers that an unexpected legacy has made her a wealthy woman and she begins to form an attachment to St John Rivers. After much persuasion, she is about to agree to marry her cousin and go to India with him on missionary work, when she mysteriously hears the voice of Rochester calling her name. She returns to find that Thornfield Hall has been burned down by Rochester's mad wife and that he has been blinded in the fire. In the final chapter, Jane and Rochester are married and begin a new life together at Ferndean Manor.

Narrative viewpoint and structure

The novel, subtitled *An Autobiography*, employs a conventional **first-person narration** and a linear chronology. Brontë's awareness of the relationship between the reader and the text is revealed in the direct address which opens the novel's final chapter: 'Reader, I married him.'

Use of Victorian context/gender/time

Like her sister Emily in *Wuthering Heights*, Charlotte Brontë presents a dark, mysterious **Byronic hero** in *Jane Eyre*: like Emily's hero, Heathcliff, Mr Rochester has a rugged, rocky name that reflects his character. Similarly, Charlotte Brontë employs a number of **Gothic** devices in her novel, such as the spooky atmosphere of Thornfield, with its unexplained cries in the night and shadowy figures glimpsed briefly on the landings. Although *Jane Eyre* is an intensely moral novel which affirms the author's Christian faith, it caused considerable controversy during the Victorian era – the second edition's dedication to the novelist William Makepeace Thackeray, for example, resulted in much gossip and speculation because Thackeray also had a mad wife! Some modern critics view *Jane Eyre* as a feminist novel; others have explored the symbolic ways in which Thornfield's destruction by fire can be linked to the other elemental forces embodied in the names of the characters Eyre, Rochester and Rivers.

2 *Wuthering Heights* by Emily Brontë (1818–1848)

This novel was published in 1847.

Biography

Of the three Brontë sisters, Emily was the most enigmatic individual and the least prolific author. Although she worked briefly as a governess and stayed for some time in Brussels with her sister Charlotte, most of her short life was spent at her father's Yorkshire parsonage. Emily's passionate attachment to the moorlands around Haworth is evident throughout her writing: it pervades both her vivid, visionary poetry and *Wuthering Heights*, her only published novel. Unlike the immediately popular *Jane Eyre*, Emily's novel received a puzzled, hostile reception from the Victorian public: one review described it as 'strange … wild, confused, disjointed, improbable'. Many modern readers might agree with this assessment, but for us these are the very features that still make the book so fascinating. Emily Brontë died of consumption within months of the publication of *Wuthering Heights*.

Story

Essentially, *Wuthering Heights* is the story of Heathcliff, allegedly an orphan picked up from the streets of Liverpool and brought back to the Heights by Mr Earnshaw. Brought up **as** one of the family, there are hints that Heathcliff **is** one of the family: he is given the name of an Earnshaw child who died in infancy and Mr Earnshaw favours this newcomer at the expense of his son Hindley. Heathcliff forms an unnaturally close bond with the daughter of the Earnshaw family, Cathy, and their wild adventures together intensify the relationship. After overhearing Cathy tell the servant Nelly Dean that 'it would degrade me to marry Heathcliff', he runs away from the Heights without listening to the end of her heartfelt confession: 'Nelly, I *am* Heathcliff – he's always, always in my mind … as my own being'. Heathcliff returns three years later to find that Cathy has married Edgar Linton of Thrushcross Grange. Nelly arranges secret meetings between Cathy and Heathcliff, but this is to be no happy reunion. Cathy dies soon after Heathcliff's return, so he begins a ruthless campaign of revenge against both the Earnshaw and Linton families. He later confesses to Nelly that he has dug up Cathy's body in order to see her one more time and, as his behaviour becomes increasingly erratic, the reader suspects that he can see Cathy's ghost – although Brontë never states this explicitly. The novel ends with the death of Heathcliff, but Brontë's conclusion is ambiguous: although a shepherd boy claims to have seen the reunited ghosts of Heathcliff and Cathy, Lockwood, the tenant who recently rented the Heights from Heathcliff, contemplates the graves of the protagonists and 'wondered how anyone could ever imagine unquiet slumbers, for the sleepers in that quiet earth'.

Narrative viewpoint and structure

Emily Brontë employs a deliberately confusing narrative **structure** in *Wuthering Heights*: a variety of **narrators**, characters with changing names, patterns repeating across generations and a shifting chronology which zigzags between the present and the past, are among the complex stylistic devices that give the novel its puzzle-like quality. For many readers, one of the thrills of reading the novel is the attempt to solve this narrative puzzle.

Use of Victorian context/gender/time

Of all the novels on the coursework reading list, *Wuthering Heights* is probably the least Victorian in terms of specific context. Many critics feel that the novel is more typical of the Gothic offshoot of **Romanticism** than of any prevailing Victorian literary trends. Marxist critics, such as Terry Eagleton, have argued that the novel is a critique of Victorian capitalism: Cathy marries Edgar only because 'he will be rich, and I shall be the greatest woman of the neighbourhood', while Heathcliff's mysterious acquisition of wealth confers unexpected power and status.

achieves a similar effect: as readers, we are left knowing more about what actually happened than any of the novel's characters do. Byatt's approach to the academics she presents is sometimes satirical: their pomposity is highlighted by her inclusion of extracts from their scholarly journals and from Mortimer Cropper's definitive Ash biography, complete with self-important footnotes.

Use of Victorian context/gender/time

Byatt's use of postmodern narrative techniques, similar to those employed in *The French Lieutenant's Woman*, enable her to offer a late 20th-century perspective on the Victorian era. Not surprisingly, her viewpoint is rather more feminist than that adopted by John Fowles in 1969. Whereas Fowles chooses to focus mainly on his male protagonist, Byatt carefully balances the lives and writing of both of her Victorian poets: for her, LaMotte's little-known fairy tales are just as important as Ash's best-selling dramatic monologues. *Possession* contains vivid re-creations of the 19th-century context: it presents the Victorian fascination with geology in considerable detail and Byatt also devotes much attention to the Victorians' interest in spiritualism.

10 *English Passengers* by Matthew Kneale (born 1960)

This novel was published in 2000.

Biography

Matthew Kneale was born in London in 1960. He read Modern History at Oxford University and there is a strong historical element in his books: like *English Passengers*, his novel *Sweet Thames* (1992) is also set in the Victorian era. *English Passengers* was first published in 2000 and won the Whitbread Book of the Year Award. It was also shortlisted for the Booker Prize for Fiction.

Story

In 1857, three Englishmen plan an expedition to confirm the Reverend Geoffrey Wilson's theory that 'the Garden of Eden was not, as supposed, located in the region of Arabia, but was instead in Australia, on the island of Tasmania'. Unfortunately, news of the colonial rebellion known as the Indian Mutiny results in their ship being requisitioned by the government. Desperate for a replacement, they charter the ironically named *Sincerity*, captained by Illiam Quillian Kewley – a Manxman who has stowed a secret cargo of smuggled brandy and tobacco between the ship's double hulls. During the voyage to Australia, there is much disagreement between the Manx crew and the English passengers (Wilson, the botanist Renshaw and the sinister Dr Potter – who hopes to test his racial theories by experimenting on the natives and collecting human specimens, once the location of Eden has been confirmed): a clash of cultures which mirrors earlier events in Tasmania. In a series of intercut flashbacks covering the previous 30 years, Kneale presents the British invasion of Tasmania and its devastating consequences. As the island's tribes are forced from their lands by white settlers and sheep farmers, many are murdered and their culture is destroyed as the British colonial system of government is imposed on the Aborigines. In the novel's later chapters, these two separate narrative strands meet: Peevay, the son of an Aboriginal woman and the European seal hunter who kidnapped her, is employed as the explorers' guide in their search for the biblical garden, and although this quest proves futile, the characters – and the reader – make other, unexpected discoveries.

Narrative viewpoint and structure

The vast narrative sweep of *English Passengers* covers the whole globe and a period of over 50 years. The novel features more than 20 different narrators, whose contributions are presented in a variety of forms: as well as direct first-person accounts, there are letters, newspaper reports, government communiqués, diary entries, reports from colonial officials, rulebooks and guidebooks. Perhaps the most distinctive of these narrative voices are Captain Kewley, Dr Potter and Peevay. Kewley speaks in the dialect of the Isle of Man: the dialect's Gaelic elements are explained in an Anglo-Manx Glossary at the end of the novel. Potter's diary is written in an amusing, semi-mathematical shorthand:

> Manxmen = treacherous even to v. last. Self heard Brew (lashed to mainmast as per usual) instructing helmsman to steer N.N.W. when self questioned he re. this he claiming we = carried into Bay of Biscay by difficult sea currents + must set course to avoid Breton Peninsular. He pointing to distant point of land to N.N.E. claiming this = Brittany. Self = doubtful.

Peevay's narrative is presented in an awkward but clear English which capitalises key ideas:

> when I finally got to his room he was more interested in wall behind me than my questionings. 'Try not to get distressed…we're doing everything we can,' but his smile said YOU ARE JUST SOME TROUBLE-MAKING BLACK FELLOW.

Use of Victorian context/gender/time

Kneale's Epilogue emphasises the contextual aspects of *English Passengers* – 'All the major events of the Tasmanian strand of the novel follow real occurrences' – and describes some of the Victorian men and women on whom he bases his characters. One of Kneale's principal themes is the Victorian response to the discoveries of contemporary geologists: confronted with the claim that Silurian limestone deposits were formed 100,000 years ago, the Reverend Wilson argues that 'the Bible tells, and with great clarity, that the earth was created a mere six thousand years ago'. The novel also addresses the issue of colonisation: Kneale believes that 'Tasmania was an example of all that was worst about the Empire… the only place where the British invasion caused the destruction of an entire culture, a whole people.' Dr Potter embodies both of these themes: his theories are a sinister synthesis of Darwinism and the racist attitudes of the colonialists – theories which, for the reader, are uncomfortably close to Nazi ideas of racial purity.

■ Writing about your chosen novel

Having reviewed all the possible choices, we are going to turn to the writing of the essay.

1 Studying the text

You will need to read your chosen novel several times so that you know and understand the text and can analyse and explore the ways the writer's choices of structure and language shape your response.

You will need to consider, discuss and make notes on the following aspects of the text:

■ the writer's purposes

■ the structure of the novel

■ the narrative viewpoint

- interesting aspects of language and imagery
- key themes
- characters.

2   Finding a focus for your essay

When you know your novel well, then, with your teacher's help, you will need to find an aspect of the text that interests you and about which you can construct an appropriate task. An appropriate task might focus on any of the aspects that you were invited to consider in the previous paragraph.

Your teacher will help you to construct a task which enables you to:

- write an informed and relevant response to your text, using coherent and accurate written expression (AO1)
- show that you can analyse the ways the writer's choices of structure and language shape meaning (AO2)
- explore your interpretation of the text (AO3)
- show your understanding of how the text reflects the Victorian context (AO4).

3   Interpretation or transformation?

Now you have another choice to make. For this essay you can:

- **either** write a conventional essay which explores some aspect of the text like characterisation, theme or structure, with a focus on your **personal informed interpretation** of the text
- **or** you can do a piece of **creative, transformational** writing such as an alternative ending, a 'missing' chapter, a letter from or diary of a character in the novel. This piece will be assessed against the same Assessment Objectives as a more conventional essay, so it will need to reflect the writer's style and the way characters are realised in the novel itself.

The following are some suggestions as to how you might approach each of these options.

The personal informed interpretation

- If your choice of novel were *Hard Times* by Charles Dickens, an appropriate task might be:

  'An exploration of the ways Charles Dickens portrays the Gradgrind and Jupe families in *Hard Times*.'

- Or, if you had chosen *Middlemarch* by George Eliot, it might be:

  'Explore the ways Eliot portrays women in *Middlemarch*.'

- Or, if you had chosen *Wuthering Heights* by Emily Brontë, it might be:

  'Examine the structure of *Wuthering Heights* and assess the impact of the structure on the ways you interpret and respond to the book.'

- Or, if you had chosen *Heart of Darkness*, it might be:

  'Explore the effects of Conrad's choice of narrator on the ways you interpret the novel.'

The creative, transformational piece

This is your opportunity to move out from the actual text and to create your own piece of writing. But remember that your writing needs to have developed from the text and to read as though it could be an integral part of it.

Activity

Write as many tasks as you can on the aspect of your chosen text that interests you. You can do this individually, with a partner, or in a group. You can then share your tasks with your partner or the group, and get your teacher to check that they are appropriate. You can also repeat this activity for your chosen drama text.

Examples of possible tasks are:

- If you had chosen to study *The French Lieutenant's Woman*, you could write a **third** alternative ending (the novel has two already).
- Or if you were studying *Hard Times*, you could compose Stephen Blackpool's diary.

💡 The drama text

Now we will turn to the second piece of writing in the coursework folder. We will begin by looking at the choices for the drama text.

There is a choice of three drama texts set for study in this coursework unit, and you will be studying **one** of them. These are the choices, in order of the time of composition.

1 *A Doll's House* by Henrik Ibsen (1828–1906)

The Norwegian writer Henrik Ibsen was one of the founders of modern drama: his plays offer a realistic presentation of the ways ordinary people are treated by society. His first plays were written in the 1860s but were not translated into English until 20 years later. Although the first London performances of several Ibsen plays caused outrage, his influence on the English theatre of the 1890s – and the next century – was immense.

A Doll's House was written in 1879 and first performed in English in 1889. Ibsen presents the audience with life in the Helmer household: a conventional Victorian marriage in which the husband is the breadwinner (Torvald is celebrating his recent promotion at the bank) and the wife's subservient role renders her little more than a doll (the affectionate nicknames by which Nora is addressed – 'my little skylark', 'my little squirrel', 'my sweet little songbird' – only serve to emphasise her insignificance). This apparently happy marriage is shattered by the revelations of the blackmailer Krogstad, who also works at the bank. When Torvald learns that Nora forged her father's signature in order to secure a loan, he rejects his wife and is concerned only for himself ('You've completely wrecked my happiness, you've ruined my whole future!') – despite the fact that the money was used to finance a cure for his near-fatal illness. Nevertheless, he insists that Nora must remain with him to maintain 'the mere façade' of a respectable marriage. Krogstad relents after he is reunited with his former lover, Nora's friend Kristine Linde, and Torvald offers to forgive his wife. But it is too late: Nora has realised that 'I've been your doll-wife...just as...I was Papa's doll-child' and that her 'sacred duty' is not to her family but 'My duty to myself.' She returns her wedding ring to Torvald and walks out of her doll's house.

Most critics see *A Doll's House* as an overtly feminist play and, although Ibsen disagreed, his notes to the play emphasise the point that 'A woman cannot be herself in contemporary society, it is an exclusively male society with laws drafted by men'. The indefinite article in the play's title implies that Nora is not the only woman in such a situation: she ultimately forces her husband to accept the fact that 'thousands of women' have made similar sacrifices. Shocked Victorian audiences saw *A Doll's House* as an attack on the sanctity of marriage, while Ibsen's scathing attitude to the materialism and hypocrisy of 19th-century society added to the play's notoriety.

Activity

Think of as many ways as you can of writing a creative, transformational task on your chosen novel. You can do this individually, with a partner or in a group. You can then share your ideas and discuss them with your teacher.

■ Writing about the chosen drama text

Having reviewed the three possible choices of drama texts, we will now turn to a consideration of the kind of task you need to construct.

1 Studying the text

You will need to read your chosen drama text several times so that you know and understand the text and can explore and analyse the ways the writer's choices of structure and language shape your responses.

You will need to consider, discuss and make notes on the following aspects of the text:

- the writer's purposes
- the structure and the setting of the play
- interesting aspects of language
- key themes
- characters.

2 Finding a focus for your essay

When you know your chosen play well, then, with your teacher's help, you will need to find an aspect of the text that interests you and about which you can construct an appropriate task. An appropriate task might focus on any of the aspects that you were invited to consider in the previous paragraph.

Your teacher will help you to construct a task which enables you to:

- write an informed and relevant response to your text, using coherent and accurate written expression (AO1)
- show that you can analyse the ways the writer's choices of structure and language shape meaning (AO2)
- explore your interpretation of the text and make connections with other texts (AO3)
- show your understanding of how the text reflects the Victorian context (AO4).

3 Comparison with the prose text or connection to other Victorian plays

Now you have another choice to make. For this essay, you can:

- **either** place the chosen play in its dramatic context, reaching out to your wider reading in Victorian drama
- **or** connect the chosen play to your chosen prose text.

Whichever task you choose, you will focus on aspects of the drama text such as theme, structure or characterisation.

- For example, if the two chosen texts were *Tess of the D'Urbervilles* and *A Woman of No Importance*, then your task might be:

  'Explore the ways Wilde presents the character of Mrs Arbuthnot in *A Woman of No Importance*.'

  Then:

  either

  – 'Compare the ways that women are presented in *A Woman of No Importance* and other Victorian plays you have read.'

  or

  – 'Compare the ways Wilde presents Mrs Arbuthnot with the ways Hardy presents Tess in *Tess of the D'Urbervilles*.'

■ Or, if the two chosen texts were *Possession* and *Arcadia*, then your task might be:

'Explore the ways Stoppard presents the relationship between the past and the present in *Arcadia*.'

Then:

either

– 'Compare the ways *Arcadia* and other Victorian plays present the influence of the past on the present.'

or

– 'Compare the ways Stoppard presents the connections between the 19th and 20th centuries with the ways Byatt presents these connections in *Possession*.'

Summary

Success in your coursework will depend on:

■ careful choice of texts

■ the negotiation of two clearly focused tasks

■ planning your time in order to make the best use of the opportunities offered by coursework

■ developing a clear line of argument

■ maintaining a focus on the writers' choices of form, structure and language

■ developing the points you make and supporting them with close reference to the text and appropriate quotation

■ your personal engagement with the texts you read and your independent thinking about them.

Who loved, who suffer'd countless ills,
Who battled for the True, the Just,
Be blown about the desert dust,
Or seal'd within the iron hills?

No more? A monster then, a dream,
A discord. Dragons of the prime,
That tare each other in their slime,
Were mellow music match'd with him.

O life as futile, then, as frail!
O for thy voice to soothe and bless!
What hope of answer, or redress?
Behind the veil, behind the veil.

CXXIII

There rolls the deep where grew the tree.
O earth, what changes has thou seen!
There where the long street roars, hath been
The stillness of the central sea.

The hills are shadows, and they flow
From form to form, and nothing stands;
They melt like mist, the solid lands,
Like clouds they shape themselves and go.

But in my spirit will I dwell,
And dream my dream, and hold it true;
For tho' my lips may breathe adieu,
I cannot think the thing farewell.

CXXIV

That which we dare invoke to bless;
Our dearest faith; our ghastliest doubt;
He, They, One, All; within, without;
The Power in darkness whom we guess;

I found him not in world or sun,
Or eagle's wing or insect's eye;
Nor thro' the questions men may try,
The petty cobwebs we have spun;

If e'er when faith had fall'n asleep,
I heard a voice 'believe no more'
And heard an ever-breaking shore
That tumbled in the Godless deep;

A warmth within the breast would melt
The freezing reason's colder part,
And like a man in wrath the heart
Stood up and answer'd 'I have felt.'

No, like a child in doubt and fear:
But that blind clamour made me wise;
Then was I a child that cries,
But, crying, knows his father near;

And what I am beheld again
What is, and no man understands;
And out of darkness came the hands
That reach thro' nature, moulding men.

Tennyson's Poetical Works, Macmillan 1911.
In Memoriam A.H.H. Cantos LIV–LVI (pp261–2) and CXXIII–CXXIV (pp282–3)

Questions

AO1: Developing an informed response to the text

■ What are the thoughts and feelings Tennyson describes in these extracts?

■ How does Tennyson see himself in these sections of the poem?

AO2: Understanding how structure, form and language shape meaning

■ What effects are created by the poetic form Tennyson uses in *In Memoriam*?

■ Tennyson wonders, 'Are God and Nature then at strife?' How does his choice of words reflect the idea of strife? You might find it useful to contrast the ways he refers to God and religion with his use of images of nature and evolution.

■ What other features of form or language do you find interesting here?

AO3: Exploring connections, comparisons and the interpretations of other readers

■ The 20th-century poet T.S. Eliot wrote of *In Memoriam*: 'Its faith is a poor thing, but its doubt is a very intense experience.' How far do you think that these extracts from the poem support his view?

■ The first three poems here are from the middle of *In Memoriam*, while the other two come near the end. What connections and comparisons can you make between the two extracts?

■ Compare the religious attitudes presented here with those you have found elsewhere in your reading of Victorian literature.

AO4: Understanding the significance and influence of contexts

■ What do these extracts show the reader about Victorian attitudes to scientific discovery?

■ What do you learn about Tennyson's Christian faith from these sections of *In Memoriam*?

Further reading

- *On the Origin of Species by Means of Natural Selection* by Charles Darwin (1859).
- *Father and Son* by Edmund Gosse (1907): Gosse's autobiography includes a vivid account of his devout father's desperate attempts to formulate convincing Christian explanations for the fossil evidence uncovered by Victorian geologists.
- *A Pair of Blue Eyes* by Thomas Hardy (1873): in Chapter 22, Henry Knight is forced to confront the significance of the fossil embedded in the cliff face from which he is hanging.
- *Dover Beach* by Matthew Arnold (1867): Arnold uses the ebbing tide as a metaphor for the 'melancholy, long, withdrawing roar' of 'The Sea of Faith' in Victorian England.
- Tennyson: *The Lady of Shallott* (1830) and *Morte d'Arthur* (1842): these Victorian versions of the legend of King Arthur were so popular that the poet later developed them into the best-selling volume *Idylls of the King* (1859).
- Tennyson: *Maud: A Monodrama* (1855): the poet called this his 'Little Hamlet' – a **dramatic monologue** in which the frequent shifts of poetic form reflect the madness of the narrator. Contemporary critics hated the poem, but for many modern readers it captures the Victorian *Zeitgeist* as effectively as *In Memoriam*.

The poetry of faith: Christina Rossetti

Although the doubts presented by Tennyson in *In Memoriam* were shared by many of his readers, it should not be forgotten that the 19th century was also an era of great religious faith.

The life and writing of Christina Rossetti (1830–94) were dominated by her Christian piety. Her relationships with several potential suitors were prematurely ended due to religious differences, and she broke off her engagement to the sculptor James Collinson when he became a member of the Roman Catholic Church. Although Rossetti lived on the fringes of a vibrant, bohemian circle of artists (her brother was the Pre-Raphaelite painter Dante Gabriel Rossetti), her life became increasingly reclusive. Despite her literary success (many Victorians felt that she should have succeeded Tennyson as Queen Victoria's Poet Laureate), Rossetti chose to stay at home with her mother and, in her later years, only left the house to attend church.

Rossetti's **dramatic monologue** *The Convent Threshold* (1862) presents a similar scenario to *Romeo and Juliet*: two lovers are about to be driven apart by a feud between their families. Unlike Juliet, however, Rossetti's speaker chooses to cut herself off from the world by entering a convent, consoling herself with the hope that she will be reunited with her lover in heaven.

Fig. 4.2 *'The Blessed Damozel' by D.G. Rossetti*

Further reading

- *The Blessed Damozel* by Dante Gabriel Rossetti (1846): this poem by Christina Rossetti's brother presents the male perspective on a situation similar to the one described in *The Convent Threshold*.
- *A Choice of Christina Rossetti's Verse* (edited by Elizabeth Jennings, 1970).
- *Christina Rossetti: A Divided Life* by Georgina Battiscombe (1981).
- The poetry of Gerard Manley Hopkins (1844–1889): various selections are available. Hopkins was a Catholic priest whose poetry often affirms his Christian faith, although – even here – Victorian doubt sometimes casts its shadow.

The poetry of obscurity: Emily Dickinson

Although most of this book attempts to place 19th-century writers in the context of their time, some readers feel that the best literature transcends time – that we should not need to know anything about a writer's background in order to enjoy what has been written. The poetry of Emily Dickinson (1830–86) might help you to decide whether you agree with this view.

Dickinson is an obscure poet in both meanings of the phrase: we know very little about her life and her poetry can sometimes be difficult to understand. We do know that she lived in Amherst, Massachusetts and that only seven of her poems were published during her lifetime. Like Emily Brontë and Christina Rossetti, Dickinson led an increasingly reclusive life: from her mid 20s she never left her house and she refused visits from anyone she did not know. It has been suggested that this eccentric behaviour was the result of a broken love affair: a speculation which some biographers believe is confirmed by the internal evidence of Dickinson's poetry. Nearly two thousand unpublished poems were discovered after Dickinson's death. Although her contemporaries were puzzled by Dickinson's poetry, open-minded modern readers are able to engage with its vivid imagery and dramatic originality.

Because most of Dickinson's poetry was never prepared for publication, her poems have no titles and we cannot be sure exactly when they were written. The likely dates of the four poems here are 1859 ('I never heard the word "escape"' and 'Bring me the sunset in a cup'), 1861 ('I'm nobody. Who are you?') and 1862 ('I heard a fly buzz when I died').

(4)
I never hear the word 'escape'
Without a quicker blood,
A sudden expectation,
A flying attitude.
I never hear of prisons broad
By soldiers battered down
But I tug childish at my bars
Only to fail again.

(16)
Bring me the sunset in a cup,
Reckon the morning's flagons up
And say how many dew,
Tell me how far the morning leaps,
Tell me what time the weaver sleeps
Who spun the breadths of blue.

Write me how many notes there be
In the new robin's extasy
Among the astonished boughs,
How many trips the tortoise makes,
How many cups the bee partakes,
The debauchee of dews.

Also, who laid the rainbow's piers,
Also, who leads the docile spheres
By withes of supple blue?
Whose finger string the stalactite,
Who counts the wampum of the
   night
To see that none is due?

Who built this little alban house
And shut the windows down so
    close
My spirit cannot see?
Who'll let me out some gala day
With implements to fly away,
Passing pomposity?

(42)

I'm nobody. Who are you?
Are you nobody too?
Then there's a pair of us.
Don't tell – they'd banish us, you
    know.

How dreary to be somebody,
How public – like a frog –
To tell your name the livelong June
To an admiring bog.

(68)

I heard a fly buzz when I died.
The stillness in the room
Was like the stillness in the air
Between the heaves of storm.

The eyes around had wrung them
    dry,
And breaths were gathering firm
For that last onset when the king
Be witnessed in the room.

I willed my keepsakes, signed away
What portion of me be
Assignable; and then it was
There interposed a fly

With blue uncertain stumbling buzz
Between the light and me;
And then the windows failed; and
    then
I could not see to see.

Selected Poems of Emily Dickinson, Heinemann 1959.
Poem numbers 4, 16, 42, 68 (pp2, 8, 23 and 41–2)

■ Further reading

Other 19th-century American texts include:

- *The Scarlet Letter* by Nathaniel Hawthorne (1850)
- *Walden* by Henry David Thoreau (1854)
- *Little Women* by Louisa M. Alcott (1868)
- *Pudd'nhead Wilson* by Mark Twain (1894)
- *The Red Badge of Courage* by Stephen Crane (1895).

■ Questions

AO1: Developing an informed response to the text

- What do you think is happening in these poems?
- What thoughts and feelings does Dickinson describe here?
- From the evidence of these four poems, what would you say are the main themes of Dickinson's writing?

AO2: Understanding how structure, form and language shape meaning

- What interests you about the ways Dickinson uses language in her poems?
- What effects are created by Dickinson's choices of form and structure?

AO3: Exploring connections, comparisons and the interpretations of other readers

- What connections can you find between Dickinson's poetry and Christina Rossetti's *The Convent Threshold*?
- Can you make any connections between Dickinson's subject matter and style and those of other 19th-century writers you have studied?
- A modern critic has claimed that Dickinson was 'a mystic visionary'. From your reading of these poems, do you agree with this view?

AO4: Understanding the significance and influence of contexts

- The seven poems by Dickinson that were published during her lifetime all appeared in a heavily edited form. Why do you think this was?
- Can you find any references to the 19th-century context in these poems?

💡 Love poetry: Elizabeth Barrett Browning

The upbringing of Elizabeth Barrett Browning (1806–61) may seem almost unbelievable to a modern reader, but it does confirm some of our stereotypes of Victorian repression. Although she was a successful poet, Elizabeth Barrett was treated like a child: she was forced to lead a sheltered life at home until the age of 40, and was forbidden to marry by her domineering father. In 1844 she began to share her views about poetry in a correspondence with Robert Browning. When they eventually met, the couple fell in love and became secretly engaged. After their clandestine marriage in 1846, the Brownings fled to Italy to escape the wrath of her father. Mr Barrett disowned his daughter: he refused ever to see her again or even to open the letters she wrote to him in the hope of reconciliation.

Sonnets from the Portuguese is a sequence of 44 poems written during the Brownings' secret courtship in 1846, but not published until 1850. Elizabeth Barrett Browning did not show these poems to her husband until after the birth of their son in 1849, possibly because of Robert Browning's distaste for so-called 'personal poetry': many of his poems are dramatic monologues, delivered by characters who are clearly not meant to be seen as versions of the poet himself. Interestingly, Robert Browning's poetry was not as popular with Victorian readers as his wife's poems were: the first edition of her 'novel-poem' *Aurora Leigh*, for instance, sold out in two weeks.

The extracts from *Sonnets from the Portuguese* printed here should give you some idea of the range of thoughts and feelings presented in the 44-poem sequence: they are **sonnets** 8, 28 and 43.

Sonnets from the Portuguese

VIII

What can I give thee back, o liberal
And princely giver, … who hast brought the gold
And purple of thine heart, unstained … untold …
And laid them on the outside of the wall
For such as I to take or leave withal,
In unexpected largesse? Am I cold,
Ungrateful … that for these most manifold
High gifts, I render nothing back at all?
Not so – not cold! – but very poor instead! –
Ask God who knows! – for frequent tears have run
The colours from my life, and left so dead
And pale a stuff, it were not fitly done
To give the same as pillow to thy head –
Go farther! – Let it serve to trample on –

XXVIII

My letters! – all dead paper, … mute and white! –
And yet they seem alive and quivering
Against my tremulous hands which loose the string
And let them drop down on my knee tonight.
This said, … he wished to have me in his sight
Once, as a friend: this fixed a day in spring
To come and touch my hand … a simple thing, …

Fig. 4.3 *"There will I ask of Christ the Lord, Thus much for him and me:–, Only to live as once on earth, With Love, – only to be, As then awhile, for ever now, Together, I and he."*

In 'The Blessed Damozel', the poet and Pre-Raphaelite painter Dante Gabriel Rossetti reverses the situation his sister presented in 'Convent Thoughts': here the female lover 'leans out from heaven'

Yet I wept for it! – This ... the paper's light ...
Said, Dear, I love thee! – and I sank & quailed
As if God's future thundered on my past.
This said, 'I am thine' – and so, its ink has paled
With lying at my heart that beats too fast.
And this ... o love, thy words have ill availed,
If, what this said, I dared repeat at last! –

XLIII

How do I love thee? Let me count the ways! –
I love thee to the depth & breadth & height
My soul can reach, when feeling out of sight
For the ends of Being and Ideal Grace.
I love thee to the level of everyday's
Most quiet need, by sun and candlelight –
I love thee freely, as men strive for Right, –
I love thee purely, as they turn from Praise;
I love thee with the passion, put to use
In my old griefs, ... and with my childhood's faith:
I love thee with the love I seemed to lose
With my lost Saints, – I love thee with the breath,
Smiles, tears, of all my life! – and, if God choose,
I shall but love thee better after my death.

Three Victorian Poets, *Cambridge University Press 1998,
Sonnets from the Portuguese, numbers VIII, XXVIII and
XLIII (pp93, 94–5, 96)*

Further reading

- *Two in the Campagna* by Robert Browning (1855): Browning did not wish his poetry to be seen as autobiographical, but the speaker in this monologue seems to be the poet himself.
- *Aurora Leigh* by Elizabeth Barrett Browning (1856).
- *Three Victorian Poets* (edited by Jane Ogborn, 1998): this excellent anthology is a useful introduction to the poetry of both Brownings, as well as Tennyson. It also includes a wealth of helpful contextual material.
- *Elizabeth Barrett Browning* by Margaret Forster (1988).
- *Lady's Maid* by Margaret Forster (1990): Forster offers a novelist's alternative to her own Browning biography.
- *Flush: A Biography* by Virginia Woolf (1933): another alternative perspective on the Brownings' relationship – from Elizabeth's pet spaniel!
- *Modern Love* by George Meredith (1862).

Questions

AO1: Developing an informed response to the text
- What are the thoughts and feelings expressed by Elizabeth Barrett Browning in these poems?
- Consider these poems as part of a sequence: do you think her feelings change or develop?

AO2: Understanding how structure, form and language shape meaning
- Why do you think Elizabeth Barrett Browning chose to use the sonnet form?
- What is your response to the language used in these poems?
- What effects are created by the poet's unusual use of punctuation here?

AO3: Exploring connections, comparisons and the interpretations of other readers
- Compare the ways Browning presents love here with the ways Rossetti presents it in *The Convent Threshold*.

- Compare Browning's sonnets with other Victorian love poems you have read.
- The opening of Sonnet 43 is one of Elizabeth Barrett Browning's most quoted lines. What other memorable declarations of love have you found in your reading of Victorian literature?

AO4: Understanding the significance and influence of contexts
- What do these poems tell you about Victorian attitudes to love and romance?
- Why do you think Elizabeth Barrett Browning chose to publish these poems under the title *Sonnets from the Portuguese*?
- From the evidence of these poems, why do you think that Elizabeth Barrett Browning's poems were so popular with Victorian readers?

■ Shropshire Lads: A.E. Housman and John Betjeman

The durability of Victorian poetry, and the persistence of its style and subject matter beyond the 19th century, can be seen in the 'Shropshire Lad' poems by A.E. Housman (1859–1936) and John Betjeman (1906–84).

Housman's *A Shropshire Lad* (1896) is a collection of 63 short lyric poems: although Housman's wistful, elegiac poetry is similar to that of John Clare or Tennyson, very few copies of the collection were sold when it was first published. Twenty years later, however, the book by this little-known writer (Housman was a university professor and only an occasional poet) became a best-seller: its nostalgic mood and yearning for lost youth struck a chord with a reading public coming to terms with the horrific slaughter of the First World War. Poems 37 and 40 of *A Shropshire Lad* are featured here.

Although some critics regard Betjeman as a literary lightweight – perhaps because of the cuddly, upper-class twit persona he cultivated for his later media work – he was a fervent admirer of the Victorians, campaigning for the preservation of Victorian architecture during the 1960s (when Gothic masterpieces such as St Pancras station were threatened with demolition) and making inventive (and occasionally surreal) use of Victorian elements in his poetry. The title of his poem 'A Shropshire Lad' (1940) is an obvious allusion to Housman, but Betjeman's Shropshire Lad is Captain Webb, the first man to swim the English Channel (in 1875).

Whereas Housman's Shropshire is an innocent rural idyll, Betjeman concentrates on the county's smokier aspects: Abraham Darby's furnaces and ironworks at Coalbrookdale were the cradle of the Industrial Revolution.

Fig. 4.4a and 4.4b *Alternative Shropshires: the iron furnaces of 'Coalbrookdale', painted by P.J. de Louthebourg in 1808 and "blue remembered hills" in 'Recollection' by J.W. Inchbold (1866)*

A Shropshire Lad

XXXVII

As through the wild green hills of Wyre
The train ran, changing sky and shire,
And far behind, a fading crest,
Low in the forsaken west
Sank the high-reared head of Clee.
My hand lay empty on my knee.
Aching on my knee it lay:
That morning half a shire away
So many an honest fellow's fist
Had well-nigh wrung it from the wrist.
Hand, said I, since now we part
From fields and men we know by heart,
For strangers' faces, strangers' lands, –
Hand, you have held true fellows' hands.
Be clean then; rot before you do
A thing they'd not believe of you.
You and I must keep from shame
In London streets the Shropshire name;
On banks of Thames they must not say
Severn breeds worse men than they;
And friends abroad must bear in mind
Friends at home they leave behind.

Oh, I shall be stiff and cold
When I forget you, hearts of gold;
The land where I shall mind you not
Is the land where all's forgot.
And if my foot returns no more
To Teme nor Corve nor Severn shore,
Luck, my lads, be with you still
By falling stream and standing hill.
By chiming tower and whispering tree,
Men that made a man of me.
About your work in town and farm
Still you'll keep my head from harm,
Still you'll help me, hands that gave
A grasp to friend me to the grave.

XL

Into my heart an air that kills
From yon far country blows:
What are those blue remembered hills,
What spires, what farms are those?

That is the land of lost content,
I see it shining plain,
The happy highways where I went
And cannot come again.

Extracts from The Collected Poems of A.E. Housman, *Cape 1977,*
Poems 37 (pp40–1) and 40 (p43)

A Shropshire Lad

N.B. – This should be recited with a Midland accent. Captain Webb, the swimmer and a relation of Mary Webb by marriage was born at Dawley in an industrial district in Salop.

The gas was on in the Institute,[1]
The flare was up in the gym,
A man was running a mineral line,
A lass was singing a hymn,
When Captain Webb the Dawley man,
Captain Well from Dawley,
Came swimming along in the old canal
That carried the bricks to Lawley.
Swimming along –
Swimming along –
Swimming along from Severn,
Andy paying a call at Dawly Bank while
    swimming along to Heaven.

The sun shone low on the railway line
And over the bricks and stacks.
And in at the upstairs windows
Of the Dawley houses' backs,
When we saw the ghost of Captain Webb,
Webb in a water sheeting.
Come dripping along in a bathing dress

To the Saturday evening meeting.
Dripping along –
Dripping along –
To the Congregational Hall;
Dripping and still he rose over the sill and faded
    away in a wall.

There wasn't a man in Oakengates
That hadn't got hold of the tale,
And over the valley in Ironbridge,
And round by Coalbrookdale,
How Captain Webb the Dawley man,
Captain Webb from Dawley,
Rose rigid and dead from the old canal
That carries the bricks to Lawley.
Rigid and dead –
Rigid and dead –
To the Saturday congregation,
Paying a call at Dawley Bank on his way to his
    destination.

[1] *"The Institute was radiant with gas."* Ch XIX, Boyhood. *A novel in verse by Rev. E. E. Bradford, D.D.*
John Betjeman's Collected Poems (*John Murray, 1958*) A Shropshire Lad (*pages 46–7*)

■ Questions

AO1: Developing an informed response to the text

■ What are the thoughts and feelings Housman expresses here?

■ What do you think is actually happening in Betjeman's poem?

AO2: Understanding how structure, form and language shape meaning

■ Explore the effects that are created by Housman's choices of language and form.

■ Explore the ways Betjeman uses images of the Victorian era in his poem.

■ What effects does Betjeman's typically Victorian use of footnotes and obscure cross-references create here?

AO3: Exploring connections, comparisons and the interpretations of other readers

■ Compare the ways in which both poets make use of Shropshire place names in their poems.

■ What other connections or contrasts can you find between these poems?

■ Can you make any links between these poems and other Victorian texts you have studied?

AO4: Understanding the significance and influence of contexts

■ Is there any evidence in these extracts to suggest why Housman's poetry became so popular during the First World War?

■ Ghost stories were very popular during Victorian times. What effects does Betjeman create by using the ghost story genre here?

■ Further reading

■ *The Invention of Love* by Tom Stoppard (1997): Stoppard presents a fictional meeting between Housman and Oscar Wilde, during which the poet guiltily reveals his feelings for his friend Moses Jackson.

■ *The Arrest of Oscar Wilde at the Cadogan Hotel* by John Betjeman (1937): the poet uses an appropriately dramatic Victorian **ballad** form here.

■ *Middlesex* by John Betjeman (1954): Betjeman namechecks minor characters from *The Diary of a Nobody* in this lament for the lost idyll of Victorian suburbia.

■ *Precious Bane* by Mary Webb (1924): the novelist mentioned by Betjeman presents a 19th-century Shropshire that is recognisable from Housman's poems.

■ *A Christmas Carol* by Charles Dickens (1843): perhaps the best-known Victorian ghost story.

■ *The Canterville Ghost* by Oscar Wilde (1887): like Betjeman, Wilde exploits the ghost story genre's potential for comedy.

💡 *Summary*

In this chapter you have looked closely at the work of six different Victorian poets. By using the chapter's questions and activities, you should have developed plenty of ideas about the style and subject matter of Victorian poetry. Before you move on to the next chapter, you should take the opportunity to check over your Poetry Reading Diary, and any other notes you have made, so that you can begin to develop an overview of 19th-century writing in this genre.

Tackling wider reading in prose

🔍 💡 Introduction

The 19th century was the golden age of the novel. Over 40,000 novels were published during the Victorian era and sales rose rapidly as educational reforms resulted in increased levels of literacy. In some ways, novels were the Victorian equivalent of today's television soap operas: many were published in weekly instalments (either separately or as features in magazines such as *Household Words* and *The Cornhill Magazine*), which included cliffhanger endings to ensure that readers bought the next episode.

Wide reading of Victorian fiction is vital if you are to succeed in the exam's context question. In your answer, you will need to use your knowledge of Victorian novels to make connections to the unprepared passage which forms the focus of the question.

💡 The realistic novel: *Anna of the Five Towns*

Bennett's first novels were set in the industrial districts of north Staffordshire known as The Potteries – which he called The Five Towns and which today form the city of Stoke-on-Trent. Bennett was born in this area and his early writing presents a realistic picture of its grim landscapes and hard-bitten inhabitants. The **realism** of *Anna of the Five Towns* (1902), however, extends beyond an evocation of the industrial setting: Bennett's realistic presentation of the novel's heroine also reveals his concerns about the position of women within Victorian society, and questions the repressive power of Victorian religious movements.

This extract marks the transition from Chapter 5 of the novel to Chapter 6. Anna has attended 'The Revival', a prayer meeting led by the evangelist Mr Banks, and, at the beginning of the extract, she speaks to an established member of the congregation, Mrs Sutton.

> 'I think I do believe,' she said weakly.
> 'You "think"? Are you sure? Are you not deceiving yourself? Belief is not with the lips: it is with the lips: it is with the heart.'
> There was a pause. Mr Banks could be heard praying.
> 'I will go home,' Anna whispered at length, 'and think it out for myself.'
> 'Do, my dear girl, and God will help you.'
> Mrs Sutton bent and kissed Anna affectionately and then hurried away to offer ministrations elsewhere. As Anna left the chapel she encountered the chapel-keeper pacing regularly to and fro across the length of the broad steps. In the porch was a notice that cabinet photographs of the revivalist could be purchased on application at one shilling each.
>
> **Chapter 6**
> Anna closed the bedroom door softly; through the open window came the tones of Cauldon Church clock, famous for their sonority and richness, announcing eleven. Agnes lay asleep under the blue-and-white counterpane, on the side of the bed next the wall, the bed-clothes pushed down and disclosing the upper half of her nightgowned figure. She slept in absolute repose, with flushed

cheek and every muscle lax, her hair by some chance drawn in a perfect straight line diagonally across the pillow. Anna glanced at her sister, the image of physical innocence and childish security, and then, depositing the candle, went to the window and looked out.

The bedroom was over the kitchen and faced south. The moon was hidden by clouds, but clear stretches of sky showed thick-studded clusters of stars brightly winking. To the far right across the fields the silhouette of Hillport Church could just be discerned on the ridge. In front, several miles away, the blast-furnaces of Cauldon Bar Ironworks shot up vast wreaths of yellow flame with canopies of tinted smoke. Still more distant were a thousand other lights crowning chimney and kiln, and nearer, on the waste lands west to Bleakridge, long fields of burning ironstone glowed with all the strange colours of decadence. The entire landscape was illuminated and transformed by these unique pyrotechnics of labour atoning for its grime, and dull, weird sounds, as of the breathings and sighings of gigantic nocturnal creatures, filled the enchanted air. It was a romantic scene, a romantic summer night, balmy, delicate, and wrapped in meditation. But Anna saw nothing there save the repulsive evidences of manufacture, had never seen anything else.

She was still horribly, acutely miserable, exhausted by the fruitless search for some solution of the enigma of sin – her sin in particular – and of redemption. She had cogitated in a vain circle until she was no longer capable of reasoned ideas. She gazed at the stars and into the illimitable spaces beyond them, and thought of life and its inconceivable littleness, as millions had done before in the presence of that same firmament. Then, after a time, her brain resumed its nightmarelike task. She began to probe herself anew. Would it have availed if she had walked publicly to the penitential form at the Communion rail, and, ranging herself with the working men and women, proved by that overt deed the sincerity of her contrition? She wished ardently that she had done so, yet knew well that such an act would always be impossible for her, even though the evasion of it meant eternal torture. Undoubtedly, as Mrs Sutton had implied, she was proud, stiff-necked, obstinate in iniquity.

Fig. 5.1 *"The repulsive evidences of manufacture." It was in scenes like this that Bennett claimed to find "the grim and original beauty of certain aspects of the Potteries"*

Agnes stirred slightly in her sleep, and Anna, aroused, dropped the blind, turned towards the room and began to undress, slowly, with reflective pauses. Her melancholy became grim, sardonic; if she was doomed to destruction, so let it be. Suddenly, half-clad, she knelt down and prayed, prayed that pride might be cast out, burying her face in the coverlet and caging the passionate effusion in a whisper lest Agnes should be disturbed. Having prayed, she still knelt quiescent; her eyes were dry and burning. The last car thundered up the road, shaking the house, and she rose, finished undressing, blew out the candle, and slipped into bed by Agnes's side.

She could not sleep, did not attempt to sleep, but abandoned herself meekly to despair. Her thoughts covered again the interminable round, and again, and yet again. In the twilight of the brief summer night her accustomed eyes could distinguish every object in the room, all the bits of furniture which had been brought from Hanbridge and with which she had been familiar since her memory began: everything appeared mean, despicable, cheerless; there was nothing to inspire. She dreamed impossibly of a high spirituality which should metamorphose all, change her life, lend glamour to the most pitiful surroundings, ennoble the most ignominious burdens – a spirituality never to be hers.

Extract from the Penguin edition, 1978, pp71–5

▪ Questions

AO1: Developing an informed response to the text

▪ What does Bennett show us about Anna Tellwright's thoughts and feelings in this extract?

▪ What impressions of Anna's relationships with other characters does the reader form here?

AO2: Understanding how structure, form and language shape meaning

▪ What effects are created by Bennett's use of an omniscient, third-person narrator in this extract?

▪ Contrast the language Bennett uses to describe Anna's surroundings here with the words he uses to present her state of mind.

▪ Consider Bennett's purposes in his use of an industrial setting in this passage. Is he merely setting the scene or does it have any importance as a symbol?

AO3: Exploring connections, comparisons and the interpretations of other readers

▪ Compare the effect of the preacher on Anna here with Kininmonth's response to Rinck's sermon in the extract from *An Abridged History* which appears later in this chapter.

▪ One of Bennett's personal literary theories was that a novelist must have 'an all-embracing compassion'. How far does he display that compassion here?

▪ In his diary, Bennett claimed that he had discovered 'the grim and original beauty of certain aspects of the Potteries'. To what extent does this passage support his claim?

AO4: understanding the significance and influence of contexts

▪ What impressions of late Victorian Britain does the reader gain from this extract?

▪ What does this passage tell the reader about the position of women in 19th-century society?

▪ From this passage, what can the reader infer about Bennett's attitudes towards religion?

▪ The novel as autobiography: *Redburn*

Some Victorian writers emphasised the realism of their novels by labelling them as **autobiographies**. *Jane Eyre* by Charlotte Brontë (1847) has the subtitle 'An Autobiography' and the full title of *Redburn* by Herman Melville (1849) is *Redburn: His First Voyage. Being the Sailor-boy Confessions and Reminiscences of the Son-of-a-gentleman, in the Merchant Service*. It is true that both books are based on the authors' own experiences: Charlotte Brontë attended a school very like Lowood, where her sister died (as Helen Burns does in the novel), and Herman Melville served on a packet ship sailing between New York and Liverpool in 1839. Nevertheless, these books are novels: by deliberately blurring the boundaries between these two genres, the authors have produced fictionalised versions of their lives, not actual autobiographies.

Herman Melville (1819–91) was probably the most important American novelist of the 19th century. He based much of his writing on his early career as a sailor. His first novels about exotic voyages in the South Seas were best-sellers, but the reading public was confused by his later, more experimental writing. His vast, complex whaling novel, *Moby Dick*, met with a hostile reception when it was first published in 1851, but is now acknowledged as one of the greatest American novels.

Redburn is a transitional novel, written between these two phases of Melville's literary career. It has a straightforward, conventional narrative structure, but it begins to grapple with some of the big spiritual and universal issues which Melville tackled in his later work. *Redburn* is of particular interest to British readers because of its American perspective on the city of Liverpool in the Victorian era. At this time Liverpool was one of the busiest and richest ports in the world, yet many of its citizens lived in horrific poverty: Melville is both fascinated and appalled by this contrast.

▪ Further reading

Other Victorian novels with industrial settings include:

▪ *Shirley* by Charlotte Brontë (1849)

▪ *North and South* by Elizabeth Gaskell (1854)

▪ *Germinal* by Emil Zola (1885)

▪ *The Necropolis Railway* by Andrew Martin (2002).

This extract is from Chapter 31 'With his prosy old guide-book, he takes a prosy stroll through the town', in which the novel's narrator goes sightseeing and reports on his impressions of the Nelson Monument which still stands in Exchange Flags, the square behind Liverpool Town Hall.

The ornament in question is a group of statuary in bronze, elevated upon a marble pedestal and basement, representing Lord Nelson expiring in the arms of Victory. One foot rests on a rolling foe, and the other on a cannon. Victory is dropping a wreath on the dying admiral's brow; while Death, under the similitude of a hideous skeleton, is insinuating his bony hand under the hero's robe, and groping after his heart. A very striking design, and true to the imagination; I never could look at Death without a shudder.

At uniform intervals round the base of the pedestal, four naked figures in chains, somewhat larger than life, are seated in various attitudes of humiliation and despair. One has his leg recklessly thrown over his knee, and his head bowed over, as if he had given up all hope of ever feeling better. Another has his head buried in despondency, and no doubt looks mournfully out of his eyes, but as his face was averted at the time, I could not catch the expression. These woe-begone figures of captives are emblematic of Nelson's principal victories; but I never could look at their swarthy limbs and manacles, without being involuntarily reminded of four African slaves in the market-place.

And my thoughts would revert to Virginia and Carolina; and also to the historical fact, that the African slave-trade once constituted the principal commerce of Liverpool; and that the prosperity of the town was once supposed to have been indissolubly linked to its prosecution. And I remembered that my father had often spoken to gentlemen visiting our house in New York, of the unhappiness that the discussion of the abolition of this trade had occasioned in Liverpool; that the struggle between sordid interest and humanity had made sad havoc at the fire-sides of the merchants; estranged sons from sires; and even separated husband from wife. And my thoughts reverted to my father's friend, the good and great Roscoe, the intrepid enemy of the trade; who in every way exerted his fine talents toward its suppression; writing a poem ('the Wrongs of Africa'), several pamphlets; and in his place in Parliament, he delivered a speech against it, which, as coming from a member for Liverpool, was supposed to have turned many votes, and had no small share in the triumph of sound policy and humanity that ensued.

How this group of statuary affected me, may be inferred from the fact, that I never went through Chapel-street without going through the little arch to look at it again. And there, night or day, I was sure to find Lord Nelson still falling back; Victory's wreath still hovering over his swordpoint; and Death grim and grasping as ever; while the four bronze captives still lamented their captivity.

Fig. 5.2 *"Nothing can exceed the bustle and activity displayed along these quays…bales, crates, boxes, and cases are being tumbled about by thousands of laborers; trucks are coming and going; dock-masters are shouting; sailors of all nations are singing out at their ropes…"*
The Liverpool waterfront in 1887, painted by Atkinson Grimshaw

Extract from the Penguin edition, 1982, pp222–3

Questions

AO1: Developing an informed response to the text

▪ Look closely at Melville's descriptions of places and people in this extract.

▪ What are the most striking features of Victorian Liverpool observed by Wellingborough Redburn?

AO2: Understanding how structure, form and language shape meaning

▪ What effects does Melville create by his use of a first-person narrator in this passage?

▪ Explore the ways Melville uses descriptive language here, paying particular attention to his use of adjectives and similes.

▪ Some critics have suggested that *Redburn* can be read as a travelogue. What effects does Melville create by using the language of his guidebook here?

AO3: Exploring connections, comparisons and the interpretations of other readers

▪ Compare the realistic ways in which Melville presents Liverpool with Bennett's realistic presentation of the Five Towns.

▪ In *Moby-Dick*, a doubloon has been nailed to the mast of Captain Ahab's whaling ship as a lucky charm. Melville devotes the whole of Chapter 98 to the different meanings that the crew find in this symbolic gold coin: as one sailor remarks, 'There's another rendering now; but still one text.' This is one of many examples in Melville's writing of what is now known as semiotics: the study of the different ways in which signs and symbols can be interpreted to make meaning. Compare Redburn's American reading of the symbolic figures on the Nelson Monument with the ways in which a 19th-century resident of Liverpool might have interpreted them.

AO4: Understanding the significance and influence of contexts

▪ What does this extract show the reader about Britain in the Victorian era?

▪ How does Melville present ideas about slavery here?

The Utopian novel: *News from Nowhere*

Although the phrase 'Victorian values' has recently been used as a slogan by politicians who seek to restore our society's allegedly lost sense of decency, morality and respect, it is worth remembering that many Victorians were unhappy with the values of their own society. While campaigning novelists, such as Charles Dickens, used their books to highlight the evils of poverty and injustice in the Britain of the 19th century, other writers were producing the blueprints for what they hoped would be a better world. Political writers such as John Ruskin and Thomas Carlyle wrote persuasively about the necessity of social change and radical reform, but perhaps the most accessible vision of a bright new future is the novel *News from Nowhere* by William Morris (1890).

William Morris (1834–96) was a 19th-century Renaissance man: an energetic and multi-talented individual who was an inspirational novelist, poet, artist, designer, publisher, entrepreneur, conservationist, environmentalist and political activist. He was a close associate of the radical group of artists known as the Pre-Raphaelite Brotherhood and was an active member of the revolutionary Socialist League.

The title of *News from Nowhere* is a direct reference to *Utopia* by Sir Thomas More (1516): a Tudor best-seller which imagined an impossibly perfect society in a country called **Utopia** (Greek for 'Nowhere'). In Morris's novel, the narrator wakes up to find himself in the year 2102 and discovers that Britain is now a harmonious society of equals who have no need for possessions, politics, schools, religion, industry, marriage or money. For Morris, the future looks like the medieval past: people have cheerfully reverted to the rural simplicities of 14th-century existence. This idealisation of the Middle Ages is a frequent feature of Victorian literature and art: it can be seen in the poetry of Tennyson, for example, as well as in the paintings of the Pre-Raphaelites and the widespread revival of Gothic architectural styles.

Further reading

▪ *Moby-Dick* by Herman Melville, particularly Chapter 98.

▪ *Wuthering Heights* by Emily Brontë, particularly Chapter 4 in which Mr Earnshaw visits Liverpool.

▪ *Her Benny* by Silas K. Hocking (1880): an almost-forgotten novel about poverty and hardship in Victorian Liverpool.

▪ *The Last Testament of Oscar Wilde* by Peter Ackroyd (1983): a 20th-century example of a novel posing as a Victorian autobiography.

This extract is taken from Chapter 3, 'Children on the Road', in which the narrator discusses education with Dick, his guide through the new world.

'Well, the youngsters here will be all the fresher for school when the summer gets over and they have to go back again.'

'School?' he said; 'yes, what do you mean by that word? I don't see how it can have anything to do with children. We talk, indeed, of a school of herring, and a school of painting, and in the former sense we might talk of a school of children – but otherwise,' said he, laughing, 'I must own myself beaten.'

Hang it! thought I, I can't open my mouth without digging up some new complexity. I wouldn't try to set my friend right in his etymology; and I thought I had best say nothing about the boy-farms which I had been used to call schools, as I saw pretty clearly that they had disappeared; and so I said after a little fumbling. 'I was using the word in the sense of a system of education.'

'Education?' said he, meditatively, 'I know enough Latin to know that the word must have come from *educere*, to lead out; and I have heard it used; but I have never met anybody who could give me a clear explanation of what it means.'

You may imagine how my new friends fell in my esteem when I heard this frank avowal; and I said, rather contemptuously, 'Well, education means a system of teaching young people.'

'Why not old people also?' said he with a twinkle in his eye. 'But', he went on, 'I can assure you our children learn, whether they go through a 'system of teaching' or not. Why, you will not find one of these children about here, boy or girl, who cannot swim, and every one of them has been used to tumbling about the little forest ponies – there's one of them now!

Fig. 5.3 *What we'll all be wearing in 2102. Dante and Beatrice: the fourteenth century as imagined by Henry Holiday in 1883*

They all of them know how to cook; the bigger lads can mow; many can thatch and do odd jobs at carpentering; or they know how to keep shop. I can tell you they know plenty of things.'

'Yes, but their mental education, the teaching of their minds,' said I, kindly translating my phrase.

'Guest,' said he, 'perhaps you have not learned to do these things I have been speaking about; and if that's the case, don't run away with the idea that it doesn't take some skill to do them, and doesn't give plenty of work for one's mind: you would change your opinion if you saw a Dorsetshire lad thatching, for instance. But, however, I understand you to be speaking of book-learning; and as to that, it is a simple affair. Most children, seeing books lying about, manage to read by the time they are four years old; though I am told it has not always been so. As to writing, we do not encourage them to scrawl too early (though scrawl a little they will), because it gets them into a habit of ugly writing; and what's the use of a lot of ugly writing being done, when rough printing can be done so easily. You understand that handsome writing we like, and many people will write their books out when they make them, or get them written; I mean books of which only a few copies are needed – poems, and such like, you know. However, I am wandering from my lambs; but you must excuse me, for I am interested in this matter of writing, being myself a fair writer.'

'Well', said I, 'about the children; when they know how to read and write, don't they learn something else – languages, for instance?'

'Of course,' he said; 'sometimes even before they can read, they can talk French, which is the nearest language talked on the other side of the water; and they soon get to know German also, which is talked by a huge number of communes and colleges on the mainland. These are the principal languages we speak in these islands, along with English or Welsh, or Irish, which is another form of Welsh; and children pick them up very quickly, because their elders all know them; and besides our guests from oversea often bring their children with them, and the little ones get together, and rub their speech into one another.'

'And the older languages?' said I.

'O yes,' said he, 'they mostly learn Latin and Greek along with the modern ones, when they do anything more than merely pick up the latter.'

'And history?' said I; 'how do you teach history?'

'Well,' said he, 'when a person can read, of course he reads what he likes to; and he can easily get some one to tell him what are the best books to read on such or such a subject, or to explain what he doesn't understand in the books when he is reading them.'

'Well,' said I, 'what else do they learn? I suppose they don't all learn history?'

'No, no,' said he; 'some don't care about it; in fact, I don't thing many do. I have heard my great-grandfather say that it is mostly in periods of turmoil and strife and confusion that people care much about history; and you know,' said my friend, with an amiable smile, 'we are not like that now.'

Extract from the Routledge edition, 1977, pp23–5

■ Questions

AO1: Developing an informed response to the text

■ What does the narrator discover about future attitudes to children and education in this extract?

AO2: Understanding how structure, form and language shape meaning

■ What effects are created by Morris's use of a question-and-answer structure in this passage?

■ Explore the ways Morris uses archaic or pseudo-medieval language here.

■ How does Morris present his ideas on the relationship between the individual and society?

AO3: Exploring connections, comparisons and the interpretations of other readers

■ Compare the liberal views on personal development expressed in this passage with the repressive forces affecting the heroine of *Anna of the Five Towns*.

■ The 1978 edition of *The Oxford Companion to English Literature* describes *News from Nowhere* as 'a romance of socialist propaganda'. To what extent does the extract support this view of Morris's novel?

■ *News from Nowhere* ends with the hope that 'if others can see it as I have seen it, then it may be called a vision rather than a dream.' How convincing do you find Morris's vision of the future?

AO4: Understanding the significance and influence of contexts

■ What does the reader learn about the Victorian 'system of teaching' from this extract?

■ How does William Morris present his own political views here?

■ Further reading

■ *Erewhon* by Samuel Butler (1872): the backward spelling of the title signals that Butler's novel is a much bleaker vision of the future, a dystopia.

■ *The Time Machine* by H.G. Wells (1895): this early example of science fiction predicts a future world of exacerbated Victorian social divisions.

■ *Selected Writings* by John Ruskin (Penguin, 1991), particularly Section 5, Society and Economics.

■ *A New and Noble School* by Quentin Bell (1982): this lucid history of the Pre-Raphaelite movement pays particular attention to Morris in Chapter 3.

■ The satirical novel: *The Diary of a Nobody*

Although Victorian literature often deals very seriously with the issues that seemed important to 19th-century readers, it would be wrong to stereotype the Victorians as grave and humourless. Dickens' novels frequently feature comical and exaggerated characters whose principal function is to amuse the reader, while the success of satirical magazines such as *Punch* (first published in 1841) also shows that the Victorians were able to laugh at themselves. *The Diary of a Nobody* by George and Weedon Grossmith (1892) began its existence as a regular column in *Punch*, becoming so popular that it was later expanded and issued in book form.

The novel reminds the 21st-century student of literature that Victorian readers did not confine themselves to serious, three-volume works of grim northern realism, nor were all Victorian writers angst-filled hermits fretting over their crises of faith and the end of the world as they knew it. The Victorian era witnessed the rapid growth of the middle classes: office clerks like the pompous Charles Pooter often lived relatively contented lives in quiet suburbs. Although the purpose of **satire** is to question society's values by highlighting its weaknesses and hypocrisies, the Grossmiths' approach is comparatively gentle. Theirs is not the vicious political mockery practised by the literary satirists of the 18th century, but an affectionate caricature which half sympathises with the menial worries of a narrator whose mundane concerns may well have been shared by their readers.

This extract is from Chapter 3 and carries the heading 'Experiments with enamel paint. I make another good joke; but Gowing and Cummings are unnecessarily offended. I paint the bath red, with unexpected result.'

> APRIL 25. In consequence of Brickwell telling me his wife was working wonders with the new Pinkford's enamel paint, I determined to try it. I bought two tins of red on my way home. I hastened through tea, went into the garden and painted some flower-pots. I called out Carrie, who said: 'You've always got some new-fangled craze'; but she was obliged to admit that the flower-pots

looked remarkably well. Went upstairs into the servant's bedroom and painted her washstand, towel-horse, and chest of drawers. To my mind it was an extraordinary improvement, but as an example of the ignorance of the lower classes in the matter of taste, our servant, Sarah, on seeing them, evinced no sign of pleasure, but merely said 'she thought they looked very well as they was before'.

APRIL 26. Got some more red enamel paint (red, to my mind, being the best colour), and painted the coal-scuttle, and the backs of our Shakespeare, the binding of which had almost worn out.

APRIL 27. Painted the bath red, and was delighted with the result. Sorry to say Carrie was not, in fact we had a few words about it. She said I ought to have consulted her, and she had never heard of such a thing as a bath being painted red. I replied: 'It's merely a matter of taste.'

Fortunately, further argument on the subject was stopped by a voice saying, 'May I come in?' It was only Cummings, who said, 'Your maid opened the door, and asked me to excuse her showing me in, as she was wringing out some socks.' I was delighted to see him, and suggested we should have a game of whist with a dummy, and by way of merriment said: 'You can be the dummy.' Cummings (I thought rather ill-naturedly) replied: 'Funny as usual.' He said he couldn't stop, he only called to leave me the Bicycle News, as he has done with it.

Another ring at the bell; it was Gowing, who said he 'must apologize for coming so often, and that one of these days we must come round to him'. I said: 'A very extraordinary thing has struck me.' 'Something funny, as usual,' said Cummings. 'Yes,' I replied; 'I think even you will say so this time. It's concerning you both; for doesn't it seem odd that Gowing's always coming and Cummings always going?' Carrie, who had evidently quite forgotten about the bath, went into fits of laughter, and as for myself, I fairly doubled up in my chair, till it cracked beneath me. I think this was one of the best jokes I have ever made.

Then imagine my astonishment on perceiving both Cummings and Gowing perfectly silent, and without a smile on their faces. After rather an unpleasant pause, Cummings, who had opened a cigar-case, closed it up again and said: 'Yes – I think, after that, I *shall* be going, and I am sorry I fail to see the fun of your jokes.' Gowing said he didn't mind a joke when it wasn't rude, but a pun on a name, to his thinking, was certainly a little wanting in good taste. Cummings followed it up by saying, if it had been said by anyone else but myself, he shouldn't have entered the house again. This rather unpleasantly terminated what might have been a cheerful evening. However, it was as well they went, for the charwoman had finished up the remains of the cold pork.

APRIL 28. Went home early and bought some more enamel paint – black this time – and spent the evening touching up the fender, picture-frames, and an old pair of boots, making them look as good as new. Also painted Gowing's walking stick, which he left behind, and make it look like ebony.

APRIL 29, SUNDAY. Woke up with a fearful headache and strong symptoms of a cold. Carrie, with a perversity which is just like her, said it was 'painter's colic', and was the result of my having spent the last few days with my nose over a paint-pot. I told her firmly that

Fig. 5.4 *"My first thought was that I had ruptured an artery, and was bleeding to death, and should be discovered, later on, looking like a second Marat, as I remember seeing him in Madame Tussaud's." Mr Pooter's red enamel paint obsession comes to an abrupt and messy end in this original illustration by Weedon Grossmith*

■ Further reading

Other Victorian novels which aim to amuse the reader include:

- *The Pickwick Papers* by Charles Dickens (1837)
- *Alice's Adventures in Wonderland* by Lewis Carroll (1865)
- *The Adventures of Tom Sawyer* by Mark Twain (1876)
- *Three Men in a Boat* by Jerome K. Jerome (1889)
- *The Card* by Arnold Bennett (1911).

I knew a great deal better what was the matter with me than she did. I had got a chill, and decided to have a bath as hot as I could bear it. Bath ready – could scarcely bear it so hot. I persevered, and got in; very hot, but very acceptable. I lay still for some time. On moving my hand above the surface of the water, I experienced the greatest fright I ever received in the whole course of my life; for imagine my horror on discovering my hand, as I thought, full of blood. My first thought was that I had ruptured an artery, and was bleeding to death, and should be discovered, later on, looking like a second Marat, as I remember seeing him in Madame Tussaud's. My second thought was to ring the bell, but remembered there was no bell to ring. My third was, that there was nothing but the enamel paint, which had dissolved with boiling water. I stepped out of the bath, perfectly red all over, resembling the Red Indians I have seen depicted at an East-End theatre. I determined not to say a word to Carrie, but to tell Farmerson to come on Monday and paint the bath white.

Extract from the Penguin edition, 1979, pp42–6

■ Questions

AO1: Developing an informed response to the text

- What impressions of Charles Pooter's character does the reader form from this extract?
- What does this passage tell us about Pooter's relationships with his wife and friends?

AO2: Understanding how structure, form and language shape meaning

- Explore the language used by the Grossmiths to present the narrator's self-importance in this extract.
- In what ways do the Grossmiths create humour here?
- What is your response to Pooter's claim that 'this was one of the best jokes I have ever made'?

AO3: Exploring connections, comparisons and the interpretations of other readers

- In what ways does this extract reflect the novel's origin as a feature in a popular magazine?
- Compare the ways the Grossmiths use ironic humour with the ways Drummond employs it in *An Abridged History*.
- The editor of the 1945 edition of *The Diary of a Nobody* claimed that it 'is a book that completely foxes the foreigner'. Why do you suppose that he made this claim? To what extent do you agree with him?

AO4: Understanding the significance and influence of contexts

- Explore the effects created by Charles Pooter's references to his possessions and his servants in this extract.
- What does the reader learn about Victorian middle-class life here?

■ The modern Victorian novel: *An Abridged History*

As a genre, the Victorian novel did not end with the death of Queen Victoria in 1901. While many of the novels published in the subsequent Edwardian era had obviously Victorian origins or settings, it is the reinvention of the Victorian novel in the second half of the 20th century that is of particular interest to students of English literature. *The French Lieutenant's Woman* by John Fowles (1969) is probably the most influential of these modern Victorian novels: its multi-layered, experimental narrative structure includes alternative endings and a range of other devices which enable the author to illuminate the presentation of his 19th-century characters with 1960s psychological and historical insights. Later developments show this genre's versatility: Fowles' novel was successfully adapted for the cinema by the dramatist Harold Pinter, while Alan Moore's graphic novel *The League of Extraordinary Gentlemen* (2001) takes an amusingly post modern approach in its teaming up of fictional Victorian heroes. The reading lists for the coursework and wider reading elements of this option include a range of modern Victorian novels; further suggestions can be found below.

An Abridged History by Andrew Drummond (2004) is a recent example of the genre: its language and form imitate the volumes of memoirs which were popular with the Victorian reading public. The novel's ironically verbose and elongated full title, *An Abridged History of the Construction of the RAILWAY LINE Between Garve, Ullapool and Lochinver; And other pertinent matters; Being the Professional JOURNAL and Regular Chronicle of ALEXANDER AUCHMUTY SETH KININMONTH*, is a deliberately exaggerated version of the sort of title seen in Melville's *Redburn*. Similarly, Drummond's use of the diary form and a pompous but naive narrator recalls *The Diary of a Nobody*. The writer develops this **pastiche** even further by including a fictional publisher's Foreword and the sort of patent medicine advertisements which adorned the endpapers of many 19th-century publications ('Stewart's Winter Fluid HEALS ALL ROUGHNESS OF THE SKIN', for example), transforming the book itself into a Victorian object.

The novel begins as a realistic account of the difficulties experienced by the engineers and navvies who constructed Victorian railway lines. Its later events become more comical and absurd as the railway is appropriated by the members of an eccentric religious sect who hope to build the New Jerusalem in the Scottish Highlands. In this extract, the narrator encounters Melchior Rinck, the founder of the sect, for the first time.

Further reading

To find out more about Pinter's film adaptation of *The French Lieutenant's Woman*, see Chapter 6.

Sunday, November 19, 1893.

I have not seen anyone from the Company since we arrived opposite Ach-na-Clerach. When Sir Cosmo Coffin came to inspect the works, McGeorge MacAdam MacAulay turned up on a cart in the company of Major Houston, and together they kept Sir Cosmo away from me as much as possible. Beyond a brief handshake and a distant smile, Coffin had no time for me, nor for the men who had performed all the hard labour to bring the railway out of Garve and in the future to bring returns on his Capital. We had had to construct a rough wooden pontoon in order that the dignitaries could cross the river from the road; her Ladyship was handed over the bridge by MacAulay with simpering looks. The man MacAulay was like a honey-bee, buzzing around Sir Cosmo and his wife with great business, while Houston speechified on the virtues of hard work and good financial sense.

We received last Thursday a brief visit from an itinerant preacher. I looked up from some work I was puzzling over and was startled to encounter, almost at my very shoulder, a most memorable figure. In appearance, he was tall, dressed as any common man in a cheap suit and stout boots. Over his right shoulder hung a voluminous black leather satchel. He wore no hat and his hair was extraordinarily white and bulky; and he had a long white beard. The whiteness was not due to senility or decrepitude, for he was about the same age as myself and gave every appearance of being muscular and strong.

He introduced himself in a voice that betrayed both American and German influences. Of Americans I am suspicious, for their habit of driving easy rail-roads across vast plains with no apparent trouble: such ease is not natural and can scarcely lead to permanence. As for Germans, I know little of them, notwithstanding the fact that my maternal uncle spent more than a year in the town of Nuremberg, studying the manufacture of biscuits. (Uncle Robert had returned from Nuremberg with all the secrets of German biscuit-making locked up in his notebooks, an optimistic slant to his hat, and dozens of lengthy and completely unintelligible words at his lips; with which latter he was used to amaze, amuse and overwhelm myself and my sister, at that time small children. Alas, our Uncle Robert had not carefully considered that the common biscuit-eating public had no inclination for his new spicy creations, despite the fashionable taste for all things German; and, after a promising first week of trading, his emporium in Dalry-road lasted no more than a few months, after which my uncle retreated in impecunious bafflement to his previous employer, Mr. McVitie of Robertson-avenue. Thereafter, only my sister and I were the grateful consumers of his German biscuits, at Christmas-time.)

The man introduced himself as 'Melchior Rinck', spelling his name carefully for me lest I get it wrong. (I would add that he persisted in calling me 'Kinnimunt', despite my polite protests.) He asked if he might sit and share bread with us. It being then noon, and my stomach being empty, I acquiesced. Within minutes I found myself engrossed in Rinck's words: he argued that if someone has never heard or seen the Bible in his whole life, then he could still have an honest Christian belief for himself, by means of the correct reception of the Spirit, just like all those who wrote the Bible without any books at all. There was no need for reverend churchmen, nor for any lawyers or politicians, for the common people could be guided by their inner torment and the Spirit alone. From such fertile ground as this, a wrathful God would be able to root out all Evil from the Earth. Some of the navvies stood around us, at a respectful distance, and were enthralled by what Rinck had to say. In truth, I too found his works oddly agitating.

At length, Rinck packed up his bag and continued on his way to Ullapool, where, as he told me, he hoped to find good ground for his message. The men drifted back to work, leaving me to muse on what Rinck had told me.

Memorandum for Mr Kininmonth: I fear I may become too reliant on the malt whisky. Gollan acquired for me (I did not ask

Fig. 5.5 *"They are a surly lot, disrespectful when I pass."*
A gang of navvies take a break during the construction of the Great Central Railway in 1896

too keenly whence) a bottle which originated in Skye, and it was in truth a very fine drop of spirit. But I have found that I take a nip out of habit, and not just when I feel low in my soul. I must put the bottle away, and cease the tippling. Perhaps it is only to be consulted on a Saturday night, when the noise of the men carousing fills me with a nameless dread and an insuperable loneliness which even the Scriptures cannot extirpate. There is much that a man can find in the Scriptures of comfort, but even more that is discomposing.

Extract from the Polygon edition, 2004, pp13–15

Questions

AO1: Developing an informed response to the text

- What are the main events recorded by Kininmonth in this journal entry?
- What thoughts and concerns does the narrator express in this extract?

AO2: Understanding how structure, form and language shape meaning

- Explore the effects created by Drummond's use of language in this extract, paying particular attention to the descriptions and the religious references.
- What effect is created by the long digression in brackets which concludes the fourth paragraph?
- In what ways does Drummond create humour in this passage?

AO3: Exploring connections, comparisons and the interpretations of other readers

- At the beginning of his journal, Kininmonth resolves to end each entry with 'a Memorandum...with some uplifting thought arising from my experiences.' How uplifting is the memorandum for 19 November 1893?
- Compare the effects created by Drummond's use of the diary form with those created by the Grossmiths in *The Diary of a Nobody*.
- Compare the ideas about religion presented by Drummond here with those presented by Bennett in *Anna of the Five Towns*.

AO4: Understanding the significance and influence of contexts

- Explore the effects created by Drummond's use of Victorian contextual detail in this passage.
- What does this passage tell the reader about Victorian attitudes to social class and to other nations?

Summary

- In this chapter you have studied extracts from five Victorian novels, written in very different styles. However, these were not the only styles of fiction that were popular in the 19th century; you should use these extracts as the starting point for your wider reading and go on to explore some of the other types of novel that were a feature of the era. You might like to begin your further investigations with ghost stories, detective fiction or the literature of Empire: these three genres were extremely popular with Victorian readers. The 'Further reading' suggestions in Chapters 4 to 7 include several different Victorian takes on the ghost story, while Arthur Conan Doyle's *Sherlock Holmes* stories are the obvious place to start for those wishing to explore detective fiction. The writing of Rudyard Kipling (1865–1936) often celebrates the achievements of the British Empire, although some of his racial views will seem offensive to students in the multicultural Britain of the 21st century. Nevertheless, he was also well aware of the Empire's potential for greed and corruption: his short story *The Man who would be King* (1888) is a compelling, succinct condemnation of irresponsible imperialism.

- As in the previous chapter, the questions and activities you have tackled here should have helped you to develop plenty of ideas about Victorian literary styles and subject matter. Once again, before you move on to the drama chapter, you should take the opportunity to update your Reading Diary – so that your thoughts about the novels you have encountered can form part of your developing overview of 19th-century literature.

Further reading

Other modern versions of the Victorian novel include:

- *Oscar and Lucinda* by Peter Carey (1988)
- *Dan Leno and the Limehouse Golem* by Peter Ackroyd (1994)
- *The Waterworks* by E.L. Doctorow (1994)
- *The League of Extraordinary Gentlemen* by Alan Moore (2001)
- *Fingersmith* by Sarah Waters (2003)
- *Arthur and George* by Julian Barnes (2006).

Tackling wider reading in drama

⚡ 💡 Introduction

As your wider reading of Victorian literature progresses, you may well find that the range of plays is much more restricted than the choices available to you in the other two literary genres. There is a historical reason for this: since 1737, when the Walpole government had passed a stage censorship law, most serious authors had abandoned the theatre for the comparative freedom of prose fiction and poetry writing. Consequently, the early Victorian repertoire consisted mainly of **melodramas**, pantomimes and 'improved' versions of Shakespeare (as actor-managers removed the dirty jokes, added extra characters and rewrote the tragedies with happy endings!). The 1843 Theatres Act increased government control over the stage so much that mid-Victorian theatre tended to rely on imported French farces and **adaptations** of popular novels (Dickens was a particular favourite with audiences).

💡 It was not until the final decades of the 19th century that drama began to be considered as serious literature. Writers including Ibsen, Wilde and Shaw attracted a new, educated, middle-class audience, as fashionable theatres mounted productions of **social drama** and sophisticated **satire**. For the working classes, there were music halls: cheap, popular variety theatres where the tradition of melodrama lived on – until the arrival of silent movies.

When you attempt the context question in the AS exam, your answer should include some relevant references to the plays you have studied, so it is important that you are familiar with a range of Victorian drama. As well as studying plays in printed form, you will find it helpful to experience them in performance. Try to see some of these plays live on stage – or, at least, on film or DVD.

A melodrama: *Maria Marten* (or *The Murder in the Red Barn*)

On 18 May 1827, William Corder murdered his lover Maria Marten in a barn in Polestead, Suffolk. After burying the body, he moved to London and married a teacher who responded to the 'Wanted' advertisement for a wife that he placed in a local newspaper. A year later, Maria's mother had a series of dreams which led to the discovery of her daughter's corpse and the arrest of William Corder. This notorious crime gripped the public imagination: a pamphlet describing the trial sold over a million copies, *The Times* devoted a quarter of its entire reporting space to the guilty verdict and ten thousand people attended Corder's execution in Bury St Edmunds (the rope used to hang him was later sold off at £1 an inch). This dramatic, true life story became a popular subject for Victorian drama, although there is a strong element of myth and folk tale to Maria Marten: there is no single definitive version of the play and we do not know the name of the original author. The play's first recorded performance was at the Marylebone Theatre, London in 1840, but there were probably earlier performances of other versions of the story.

Melodrama was a staple of early Victorian theatre: its sensational, crowd-pleasing mixture of romance, violence, **comedy** and music provided cheap entertainment for ordinary working people. There was an element of pantomime about this form of drama: these popular, simple plays drew large audiences who expected to see action-packed stories about characters that we might now regard as mere stereotypes. They are the sort of characters who are still recognisable to us, however, even if we might now think of them as clichés: the moustache-twirling villain (like Dick Dastardly, or the men who tie women to railway lines in silent movies); the innocent country maid who is the victim of this wicked seducer; the mysterious gypsy with his all-seeing eye.

These scenes from Act Two of Maria Marten are taken from the version written by John Latimer for the Queen's Theatre, Battersea. In the first, Corder, having murdered their illegitimate baby, helps Maria to bury the child's body in a wood; in the second, he murders the only witness to the burial.

Scene Four

A secret part of the wood.
William and Maria discovered burying the child.

Maria William, William, this is a fearful deed.

Corder But it must be done for both our safeties.

Maria My poor infant, to be buried like a dog, no prayers above its little head, far from the shadow of the Church, to leave it here within this Wood it's terrible.

Corder 'Tis for the best, believe me. An inquest might tell more than we should like the world to know.

Maria Ah? Then the child has not come to its sudden death by fair means?

Corder How should I know, if a mistake has been made, it lies with the doctor not myself.

Maria Oh! What horrible suspicions cross my mind!

Corder Then let suspicion die, for a magistrate's enquiry would harm you more than myself. Remember the penalty of concealment of birth.

Maria I am in your power and have no will of my own, but it's hard for my little one to be here.

Corder Nonsense, the child will sleep peaceful as in a Churchyard. See, I have marked this tree so that at eventide you can strew the little grave with flowers.

Maria Oh, take me, take me quickly from this fearful spot.

Corder Come then, how you tremble! Nonsense, girl! No eye beholds us.

Ishmael (*In the distance*) Yes, the eye of Ishmael the Gipsy.

Scene Six

A farm yard. Enter Gipsies with torches.

Mark This way brothers, I hear the servants are in the village, Corder is from home. Now's our time. But should he return, we hurl him into the blazing fire. Remember, dead men tell no tales, this way, this way.

They go behind the Farm buildings

Enter **Ishmael**.

Ishmael Brave boys, there at their work, soon all will be a heap of ruin, ha, ha. The Farm in darkness, where can Corder be?

*Enter **Corder** with a gun.*

Corder Here old traitor, Dog – villain you would betray me.

Ishmael Aye, I would drive you a beggar from your home.

Corder Ah, ah, that threat I laugh at, the Farm and all's insured to its full value so they can go to the devil.

Ishmael But your life is in my power. I am the father of that poor girl whose soul you so basely betrayed, the father of the lad you drove to exile, I swore revenge, it is at hand. I dogged you step by step, I saw you poison Maria's child and bury it in the woods, I will take the officers there and your life is forfeit.

Corder So is yours old traitor. (*Shoots him.*) So perish the only witness to my crime.

Exit hurriedly.

Enter Gipsies with torches.

Mark That shot, ah, see our father bleeds! (*They raise him.*) Who has done this?

Ishmael William Corder. I am dying. Swear to seek out my son, swear by the mystic relics of our tribes, tell him to relentlessly pursue the path of vengeance until mine and his sister's death are avenged.

All We swear.

Ishmael 'Tis well, 'tis well, my eyes grow dim. My blood is chilled and see, the spirit of my Zella calls to my home among the stars.

Mark But this secret you know of Corder's, reveal it to us ere you die.

Corder Corder, he is – a … (*falls back*).

Mark The spirit is struggling to break from its earthy prison but the doors are fast, while we hang over him, our brother is in his death throes but the reluctant spirit cannot pass away, the stars have gone out, and the moon has veiled her face, lift up your voices and let every face look steadily to the WEST.

*During this speech there are heard the first bars of a solemn dirge. The Gipsies kneel round **Ishmael** who leans his dying head on **Mark's** shoulder. The stage is lighted only by the red glare of the burning Farm. The Gipsies sing:*

Fig. 6.1 *"The eye of Ishmael the Gipsy." In this Victorian engraving, Corder and Maria are discovered burying their illegitimate baby in the wood*

Let the dirge be sung
And the bell be rung
And the torch burn red
O'er the dying one's head
Till the spirit is free
And the flesh is dead.
Troubled spirit pass away
From your prison house of clay,
Every door is open wide.
Night is at the turn of tide.
Pass away,
Pass away.

Darkness creeps over the scene.

CURTAIN

Extract from Maria Marten, *Heinemann 1971.*
Act Two, Scenes 4–6, pp25 and 28–30

Questions

AO1: Developing an informed response to the text

- What happens in these scenes?
- What are your thoughts and feelings about the characters in this extract?

AO2: Understanding how structure, form and language shape meaning

- Why do you think writer of this play has used such short scenes?
- How does the language used by these characters affect the audience's response to them?
- Explore the dramatic effects that are created in this extract. You might find it useful to look at the stage directions and to consider why the writer has included the gypsies' song.

AO3: Exploring connections, comparisons and the interpretations of other readers

- Compare the presentation of Maria Marten in Scene Four with the ways women are presented in the other extracts in this chapter.
- To what extent do you think that Corder is presented as a stereotypical Victorian villain here?

AO4: Understanding the significance and influence of contexts

- From the evidence of these scenes, why do you think that *Maria Marten* was such a popular play with Victorian audiences?
- What does this extract tell you about Victorian ideas of justice and morality?
- What do these scenes tell you about 19th-century attitudes to gypsies and their culture?

Further reading

In the chapter of his autobiography which recalls his education at Oxford University, John Ruskin wrote that he would have preferred to be 'beside a gipsy's kettle on Addington Hill (not that I had ever been beside a gipsy's kettle, but often wanted to be)'. Victorian writers often presented gypsies as enviable figures: their way of life represented a freedom from conventional responsibilities and the rigid expectations of 19th-century society. This view of Romany culture is evident in *Maria Marten* and can also be found in texts such as:

- *The Gypsies' Evening Blaze* (1820), *The Gipsies* (1835) and *The Gypsy Camp* (1841) by John Clare
- *Jane Eyre* by Charlotte Brontë (1847), especially Chapters 18 and 19
- *Lavengro* (1851) and *The Romany Rye* (1857) by George Borrow
- *The Scholar Gypsy* by Matthew Arnold (1853)
- *The Adventure of the Speckled Band* by Arthur Conan Doyle (1898).

■ A comedy: *The Admirable Crichton*

Although his literary career began with a series of now largely forgotten novels in the last two decades of the 19th century, J.M. Barrie (1860–1937) is best known today as the author of *Peter Pan* (1904). It would be a mistake, however, to judge Barrie's writing on the basis of its over-familiar, Disneyfied and sanitised representations: far from being the syrupy children's story popularised in cartoon versions, the original Peter Pan is a much darker work, full of slyly satirical comment on the values of late Victorian society. Similarly, Barrie's first commercially successful play, *The Admirable Crichton* (written at the end of the Victorian era and first performed in 1902), contains much serious social comment beneath its comic surface.

Fig. 6.2 *Even butlers have feelings. Love among the servants in 'The Garden of Eden' by Briton Riviere (1901)*

The Admirable Crichton is a sort of Victorian *Lord of the Flies*. The play opens in the Mayfair residence of Lord Loam, a progressive aristocrat who believes that 'our divisions into classes are artificial, that if we were return to Nature, all would be equal'. His theories are tested in the play's subsequent acts: when his yacht is shipwrecked in the Pacific, his party of English aristocrats and their servants are forced to live on a desert island. Here, 19th-century class distinctions quickly disappear and the social order is inverted: in the Darwinian struggle for survival, Crichton the butler turns out to be the member of the party who is best equipped to succeed. This was, of course, very amusing and entertaining for Barrie's middle-class theatre audience, but there is more to the play than this: Barrie is not merely supplying laughter to the theatre-going public, but also posing important questions about the nature and effects of class divisions in Victorian society.

At the beginning of this extract from Act Two of *The Admirable Crichton*, The Honourable Ernest Woolley has been given a humiliating soaking, at the orders of Lord Loam.

> **Lord Loam** (*loftily, from the door of the hut*) Have you carried out my instructions, Crichton?
> **Crichton** (*deferentially*) Yes, my lord.
> (*Ernest appears, mopping his hair, which has become very wet since we last saw him. He is not bearing malice, he is too busy drying, but Agatha is specially his champion*)
> **Agatha** It's infamous, infamous.
> **Lord Loam** (*strongly*) My orders, Agatha.
> **Lady Mary** Now, father, please.
> **Lord Loam** (*striking an attitude*) Before I give you any further orders, Crichton –
> **Crichton** Yes, my lord.
> **Lord Loam** (*delighted*) Pooh! It's all right.
> **Lady Mary** No. Please go on.
> **Lord Loam** Well, well. This question of the leadership; what do you think now, Crichton?

Crichton My lord, I feel it is a matter with which I have nothing to do.

Lord Loam Excellent. Ha, Mary? That settles it, I think.

Lady Mary It seems to, but – I'm not sure.

Crichton It will settle itself naturally, my lord, without any interference from us.

(*The reference to Nature gives general dissatisfaction*)

Lady Mary Father.

Lord Loam (*a little severely*) It settled itself long ago, Crichton, when I was born a peer, and you, for instance, were born a servant.

Crichton (*acquiescing*) Yes, my lord, that was how it all came about quite naturally in England. We had nothing to do with it there, and we shall have as little to do with it here.

Treherne (*relieved*) That's all right.

Lady Mary (*determined to clinch the matter*) One moment. In short, Crichton, his lordship will continue to be our natural head.

Crichton I dare say, my lady, I dare say.

Catherine But you must know.

Crichton Asking your pardon, my lady, one can't be sure – on an island.

(*They look at each other uneasily*)

Lord Loam (*warningly*) Crichton, I don't like this.

Crichton (*harassed*) The more I think of it, your lordship, the more uneasy I become myself. When I heard, my lord, that you had left that hairpin behind –

(*He is pained*)

Lord Loam (*feebly*) One hairpin among so many would only have caused dissension.

Crichton (*very sorry to have to contradict him*) Not so, my lord. From that hairpin we could have made a needle; with that needle we could, out of skins, have sewn trousers – of which your lordship is in need; indeed, we are all in need of them.

Lady Mary (*suddenly self-conscious*) All?

Crichton On an island, my lady.

Lady Mary Father.

Crichton (*really more distressed by the prospect than she*) My lady, if Nature does not think them necessary, you may be sure she will not ask you to wear them. (*Shaking his head*) But among all this undergrowth –

Lady Mary Now you see this man in his true colours.

Lord Loam (*violently*) Crichton, you will either this moment say, 'Down with Nature,' or –

Crichton (*scandalised*) My lord!

Lord Loam (*loftily*) Then this is my last word to you; take a month's notice.

(*If the hut had a door he would now shut it to indicate that the interview is closed*)

Crichton (*in great distress*) Your lordship, the disgrace –

Lord Loam (*swelling*) Not another word: you may go.

Lady Mary (*adamant*) And don't come to me, Crichton, for a character.

Ernest (*whose immersion has cleared his brain*) Aren't you forgetting that this is an island?

(*This brings them to earth with a bump. Lord Loam looks to his eldest daughter for the fitting response*)

Lady Mary (*equal to the occasion*) It makes only this difference
– that you may go at once, Crichton, to some other part of the
island.

(*The faithful servant has been true to his superiors ever since he
was created, and never more true than at this moment; but his
fidelity is founded on trust in Nature, and to be untrue to it would
be to be untrue to them. He lets the wood he has been gathering
slip to the ground, and bows his sorrowful head. He turns to obey.
Then affection for these great ones wells up in him*)

Crichton My lady, let me work for you.

Lady Mary Go.

Crichton You need me so sorely; I can't desert you; I won't.

Lady Mary (*in alarm, lest the others may yield*) Then, father, there
is but one alternative, we must leave him.

(*Lord Loam is looking yearningly at Crichton*)

Treherne It seems a pity.

Catherine (*forlornly*) You will work for us?

Treherne Most willingly. But I must warn you all that, so far,
Crichton has done nine-tenths of the scoring.

Lady Mary The question is, are we to leave this man?

Lord Loam (*wrapping himself in his dignity*) Come, my dears.

Crichton My lord!

Lord Loam Treherne – Ernest – get our things.

Ernest We don't have any, uncle. They all belong to Crichton.

Treherne Everything we have he brought from the wreck – he went
back to it before it sank. He risked his life.

Crichton My lord, anything you would care to take is yours.

Lady Mary (*quickly*) Nothing.

Ernest Rot! If I could have your socks, Crichton –

Lady Mary Come, father; we are ready.

(*Followed by the others, she and Lord Loam pick their way up the
rocks. In their indignation they scarcely notice that daylight is
coming to a sudden end*)

Crichton My lord, I implore you – I am not desirous of being head.
Do you have a try at it, my lord.

Lord Loam (*outraged*) A try at it!

Crichton (*eagerly*) It may be that you will prove to be the best man.

Lord Loam May be! My children, come.

(*They disappear proudly but gingerly up those splintered rocks*)

Treherne Crichton, I'm sorry; but of course I must go with them.

Crichton Certainly, sir.

(*He calls to Tweeny, and she comes from behind the hut, where she
has been watching breathlessly*)

Will you be so kind, sir, as to take her to the others.

Treherne Assuredly.

Tweeny But what do it all mean?

Crichton Does, Tweeny, does. (*He passes her up the rocks to
Treherne*) We shall meet again soon, Tweeny. Good-night, sir.

Treherne Good-night. I dare say they are not far away.

Crichton (*thoughtfully*) They went westward, sir, and the wind
is blowing in that direction. That may mean, sir, that Nature
is already taking the matter into her own hands. They are all
hungry, sir, and the pot has come a-boil. (*He takes off the lid*)
The smell will be borne westward. That pot is full of Nature, Mr
Treherne. Good-night, sir.

Treherne Good-night.

(He mounts the rocks with Tweeny, and they are heard for a little time after their figures are swallowed up in the fast growing darkness. Crichton stands motionless, the lid in his hand, though he has forgotten it and his reason for taking it off the pot. He is deeply stirred, but presently is ashamed of his dejection, for it is as if he doubted his principles. Bravely true to his faith that Nature will decide now as ever before, he proceeds manfully with his preparations for the night. He lights a ship's lantern, one of several treasures he has brought ashore, and is filling his pipe with crumbs of tobacco from various pockets, when the stealthy movement of some animal in the grass startles him. With the lantern in one hand and his cutlass in the other, he searches the ground around the hut. He returns, lights his pipe, and sits down by the fire, which casts weird moving shadows. There is a red gleam on his face; in the darkness he is a strong and perhaps rather sinister figure. In the great stillness that has fallen over the land, the wash of the surf seems to have increased in volume. The sound is indescribably mournful. Except where the fire is, desolation has fallen on the island like a pall.

Once or twice, as Nature dictates, Crichton leans forward to stir the pot, and the smell is borne westward. He then resumes his silent vigil.

Shadows other than those cast by the fire begin to descend the rocks. They are the adventurers returning. One by one they steal nearer to the pot until they are squatted round it, with their hands out to the blaze. Lady Mary only is absent. Presently she comes within sight of the others, then stands against a tree with her teeth clenched. One wonders, perhaps, what Nature is to make of her)

Extract from The Admirable Crichton, *OUP 1995, pp36–8*

Further reading

Other Victorian comedies include:

- *Money* by Edward Bulwer-Lytton (1840)
- *London Assurance* by Dion Boucicault (1841)
- *Charley's Aunt* by Brandon Thomas (1892)
- *The Importance of Being Earnest* by Oscar Wilde (1895)
- *Trelawny of the 'Wells'* by Arthur Wing Pinero (1898)
- *Hobson's Choice* by Harold Brighouse (1915).

Questions

AO1: Developing an informed response to the text

- What are the main events in this extract?
- What are your thoughts and feelings about the characters Barrie presents here?

AO2: Understanding how structure, form and language shape meaning

- How does Barrie present the character of Crichton in this extract? Does he seem 'admirable' to you?
- Explore the ways Barrie makes use of stage directions, especially the one which concludes this second act of the play.
- How does Barrie create both conflict and comedy in this extract?
- What interests you about the ways that Barrie uses language here?

AO3: Exploring connections, comparisons and the interpretations of other readers

- When Tweeny is introduced in Act One, the audience learns that she is 'not, at present, strictly speaking, anything; a *between* maid'. How does Barrie develop this idea in the extract from Act Two?
- Contrast Barrie's presentation of Treherne (who is a clergyman) with the behaviour of the other members of Lord Loam's party. Why do you think the writer has made this distinction?
- In an early review of this play, the theatre critic of the *New York Times* wrote that he was unsure 'whether Barrie was writing comedy or a lucubration of the woes of the world'. From your reading of this extract, which do *you* think Barrie was writing?

AO4: Understanding the significance and influence of contexts

- What does this extract show you about Victorian attitudes to social class?
- How does Barrie present contemporary ideas about etiquette and codes of behaviour?

■ A banned play: *Mrs Warren's Profession*

Strict Victorian beliefs about decency and morality meant that 19th-century literature was often subjected to censorship. In your reading, you may have noticed that publishers considered the word 'damn' such an unprintable blasphemy that it is sometimes shown as 'd---' in Victorian novels. Similarly, as explained in the Introduction to this chapter, Victorian theatres were tightly regulated: a play needed to be granted a licence by the Lord Chamberlain, the government's official censor, before it could be performed in public. When a play was refused a performance licence, its author either had to rewrite it or accept that the play would probably never make it onto the stage at all.

Mrs Warren's Profession by George Bernard Shaw (1856–1950) was written in 1893 and first appeared in print in 1898. Shaw told the theatre director J.T. Grein that 'I do not think there is the least chance of the play being licensed', and its first public performance took place in America in 1905 – when a warrant was issued for the arrest of the entire cast and stage crew! In England, the play was not performed in public until 1925: the year Shaw was awarded the Nobel Prize for Literature. The play caused so much outrage because of the profession to which its title refers (Mrs Warren used to be a prostitute; now she manages a chain of high-class continental brothels), but the controversy was exacerbated by Shaw's introduction of the equally taboo subject of incest.

Shaw was a prolific dramatist (during his literary career he wrote over fifty plays) and a radical freethinker: his socialist and feminist views were considered extreme during the late Victorian era. Inspired by the work of Ibsen, Shaw used his plays to confront British audiences with the moral and social problems of his time.

In this extract from Act Two of *Mrs Warren's Profession*, Vivie Warren discovers that her education at a private boarding school and Cambridge University has been funded by her mother's immoral earnings.

Mrs Warren (*piteously*) Oh, my darling, how can you be so hard on me? Have I no rights over you as your mother?
Vivie Are you my mother?
Mrs Warren (*appalled*) Am I your mother? Oh, Vivie!
Vivie Then where are our relatives? my father? our family friends? You claim the right of a mother: the right to call me fool and child; to speak to me as no other woman in authority over me at college dare to speak to me; to dictate my way of life; and to force on me the acquaintance of a brute whom any one can see to be the most vicious sort of London man about town. Before I give myself the trouble to resist such claims, I may as well find out whether they have any real existence.
Mrs Warren (*distracted, throwing herself on her knees*) Oh no, no. Stop, stop. I am your mother, I swear it. Oh, you can't mean to turn on me – my own child! It's not natural. You believe me, don't you? Say you believe me.
Vivie Who was my father?
Mrs Warren You don't know what you are asking. I can't tell you.
Vivie (*determinedly*) Oh yes you can, if you like. I have a right to know; and you know very well that I have that right. You can refuse to tell me, if you please; but if you do you will see the last of me tomorrow morning.
Mrs Warren Oh, it's too horrible to hear you talk like that. You wouldn't – you couldn't leave me.

Vivie (*ruthlessly*) Yes, without a moment's hesitation, if you trifle with me about this. (*Shivering with disgust*) How can I feel sure that I may not have the contaminated blood of that brutal waster in my veins?

Mrs Warren No, no. On my oath it's not he, nor any of the rest that you have ever met. I'm certain of that, at least.

Vivie's eyes fasten sternly on her mother as the significance of this flashes on her.

Vivie (*slowly*) You are certain of that, at least. Ah! You mean that that is all you are certain of. (*Thoughtfully*) I see. (*Mrs Warren buries her face in her hands*) Don't do that, mother: you know you don't feel it a bit.

[…]

Mrs Warren D'you know what your gran'mother was?

Vivie No

Mrs Warren No, you don't. I do. She called herself a widow and had a fried-fish shop down by the Mint, and kept herself and four daughters out of it. Two of us were sisters: that was me and Liz; and we were both good-looking and well made. I suppose our father was a well-fed man: mother pretended he was a gentleman; but I don't know. The other two were only half sisters: undersized, ugly, starved looking, hard working, honest poor creatures: Liz and I would have half-murdered them if mother hadn't half-murdered us to keep our hands off

Fig. 6.3 *"All we had was our appearance and our turn for pleasing men." 'The Awakening Conscience' by William Holman Hunt (1853) shows the moment when, unlike Mrs Warren, a "kept woman" realises the error of her ways*

them. They were the respectable ones. Well, what did they get by their respectability? I'll tell you. One of them worked in a whitelead factory twelve hours a day for nine shillings a week until she died of lead poisoning. She only expected to get her hands a little paralyzed; but she died. The other was always held up to us a model because she married a Government laborer in the Deptford victualling yard, and kept his room and the three children neat and tidy on eighteen shillings a week – until he took to drink. That was worth being respectable for, wasn't it?

Vivie (*now thoughtfully attentive*) Did you and your sister think so?

Mrs Warren Liz didn't, I can tell you: she had more spirit. We both went to a church school – that was part of the ladylike airs we gave ourselves to be superior to the children that knew nothing and went nowhere – and we stayed there until Liz went out one night and never came back. I know the schoolmistress thought I'd soon follow her example; for the clergyman was always warning me that Lizzie'd end by jumping off Waterloo Bridge. Poor fool: that was all he knew about it! But I was more afraid of the whitelead factory than I was of the river; and so would you have been in my place. That clergyman got me a situation as scullery maid in a temperance restaurant where they sent out for anything you liked. Then I was a waitress; and then I went to the bar at Waterloo station: fourteen hours a day serving drinks and washing glasses for four shillings a week and my board. That was considered a great promotion for me. Well, one cold, wretched night, when I was so tired I could hardly keep myself awake, who should come up for a half of scotch but Lizzie, in a long fur cloak, elegant and comfortable, with a lot of sovereigns in her purse.

Vivie (*grimly*) My aunt Lizzie!

Mrs Warren Yes; and a very good aunt to have, too. She's living down at Winchester now, close to the cathedral, one of the most respectable ladies there. Chaperones girls at the county ball, if you please. No river for Liz, thank you! you remind me of Liz a little: she was a first-rate business woman – saved money from the beginning – never let herself look too like what she was – never lost her head or threw away a chance. When she saw I'd grown up good-looking she said to me across the bar 'What are you doing there, you little fool? wearing out your health and your appearance for other people's profit!' Liz was saving money then to take a house for herself in Brussels; and she thought we two could save faster than one. So she lent me some money and gave me a start; and I saved steadily and first paid her back, and then went into business with her as her partner. Why shouldn't I have done it? The house in Brussels was real high class: a much better place for a woman to be in than the factory where Anne Jane got poisoned. None of our girls were ever treated as I was treated in the scullery of that temperance place, or at the Waterloo bar, or at home. Would you have had me stay in them and become a worn-out old drudge before I was forty?

Vivie (*intensely interested by this time*) No, but why did you choose that business? Saving money and good management will succeed in any business.

Mrs Warren Yes, saving money. But where can a woman get the money to save in any other business? Could you save out of four shillings a week and keep yourself dressed as well? Not you. Of course, if you're a plain woman and can't earn anything more; or if you have a turn for music, or the stage, or newspaper-writing: that's different. But neither Liz nor I had any turn for such things: all we had was our appearance and our turn for pleasing men. Do you think we were such fools as to let other people trade in our good looks by employing us as shopgirls, or barmaids, or waitresses, when we could trade in them ourselves and get all the profits instead of starvation wages? Not likely.

Vivie You were certainly quite justified – from the business point of view.

Mrs Warren Yes; or any other point of view. What is any respectable girl brought up to do but catch some rich man's fancy and get the benefit of his money by marrying him? – as if a marriage ceremony could make any difference in the right or wrong of the thing! Oh, the hypocrisy of the world makes me sick!

Extract from Mrs Warren's Profession, *Broadview edition 2005, pp118–24*

■ Questions

AO1: Developing an informed response to the text

■ What does this extract tell you about the story of Mrs Warren's life?

■ What are your thoughts and feelings about the characters of Mrs Warren and Vivie?

AO2: Understanding how structure, form and language shape meaning

■ What do you notice about the way Shaw structures the dialogue in this extract?

■ How does the language used by these two characters affect the audience's response to them?

■ Explore the dramatic effects that Shaw creates in this extract. You might find it helpful to look closely at his use of stage directions.

AO3: Exploring connections, comparisons and the interpretations of other readers

■ In a review of this play's first performance, the *New York Herald* claimed that 'the characters are wholly immoral and degenerate'. To what extent do you agree with this view?

■ Some critics feel that Shaw's characters are unconvincing because they are merely vehicles for his political views. Having read the extract, do you think this is true?

■ Contrast Shaw's presentation of these two women: what are the differences between them?

AO4: Understanding the significance and influence of contexts

■ What does this extract tell you about the position of women in Victorian society?

■ From the evidence of this extract, why do you think the Lord Chamberlain refused this play a performance licence?

■ Shaw advocated the reform of English spelling and punctuation. What evidence of this can you find in the extract? Do you think it makes any difference?

■ Further reading

Other banned or highly controversial Victorian texts include:

■ *Leaves of Grass* by Walt Whitman (1855–91): Whitman's first publisher caved in when the attorney for the New England Society for the Suppression of Vice informed him that 'the provisions of the Public Statutes respecting obscene literature suggest the propriety of withdrawing and suppressing editions' of *Leaves of Grass*. The ensuing publicity increased sales of the book once Whitman had found a new publisher.

■ *Ghosts* by Henrik Ibsen (1881): Victorian audiences were not ready for a play about the corrosive effects of syphilis.

■ *The Complete Works of Emile Zola*: in 1889, legal action by the National Vigilance Association resulted in three months' imprisonment for the publisher Henry Vizetelly when he refused to comply with an injunction to 'withdraw all translations of M. Zola's work from circulation'.

■ *The Second Mrs Tanqueray* by Arthur Wing Pinero (1893): like Mrs Warren, Mr Tanqueray's new wife has a shady past which will return to haunt her.

■ *The Picture of Dorian Gray* by Oscar Wilde (1891): the *Scots Observer* claimed that this novel was suitable 'for none but outlawed noblemen and perverted telegraph boys'.

■ *Salome* by Oscar Wilde (1894): banned in Britain until 1927.

■ *Jude the Obscure* by Thomas Hardy (1895): this book met with a unanimously hostile reception, which effectively ended Hardy's career as a novelist.

A play in translation: *Three Sisters*

Anton Chekhov's play *The Seagull* (1895) received its first English performance in 1909, quickly followed by translated versions of his plays *Uncle Vanya* (first performed in Russia, 1900), *Three Sisters* (1901) and *The Cherry Orchard* (1904). Although Chekhov's uneventful world of repressed 19th-century upper middle-class Russians may seem rather remote to 21st-century A-level students, these plays have remained extremely popular and Chekhov has been a continuing influence on modern drama in both Europe and America.

The events of *Three Sisters* take place in a garrison town, somewhere in the remote provinces of northern Russia. Both of the Act One extracts below are taken from Michael Frayn's 1983 translation of the play. In the first extract, the three sisters – Olga, Masha and Irina – welcome Doctor Chebutykin, the medical officer, and Lieutenant Baron Tusenbach to the Prozorov family home; in the second, the newly arrived Lieutenant-Colonel Vershinin introduces himself to the family.

Don't let yourself be put off by the names! For the purposes of your wider reading, it is what the characters talk about and the ways Chekhov presents it that are important.

Irina Ivan Romanich! Dear Ivan Romanich!

Chebutykin My little girl! What is it, my precious?

Irina Tell me, why am I so happy today? As if I were sailing, with the wide blue sky above me, and great white birds soaring in the wind. Why is it? Why?

Chebutykin (*kissing both her hands, tenderly*) My own white bird …

Irina I woke up this morning, I got up, I washed – and suddenly I felt everything in this world was clear to me – I felt I knew how life had to be lived. Dear Ivan Romanich, I can see it all. A human being has to labour, whoever he happens to be, he has to toil in the sweat of his face; that's the only way he can find the sense and purpose of his life, his happiness, his delight. How fine to be a working man who rises at first light and breaks stones on the road, or a shepherd, or a teacher, or an engine driver on the railway … Lord, never mind being human even – better to be an ox, better to be a simple horse, just so long as you work – anything rather than a young lady who rises at noon, then drinks her coffee in bed, then takes two hours to dress … that's terrible! In hot weather sometimes you long to drink the way I began longing to work. And if I don't start getting up early and working, then shut your heart against me, Ivan Romanich.

Chebutykin (*tenderly*) I'll shut it, I'll shut it tight.

Olga Father trained us to rise at seven. Now Irina wakes at seven and lies there till nine o'clock at least, just thinking. She looks so serious, though! (*Laughs*)

Irina You're used to seeing me as a child, so then you find it odd when I look serious. I'm twenty!

Tusenbach A longing to work – oh, heavens, how well I know that feeling! I've never done a stroke of work in my life. I was born in Petersburg, that cold and idle city, and none of my family had ever known what it was to work, they'd never known care. When I used to come home from cadet school a servant would pull my boots off for me, while I played the fool. My mother regarded me with an indulgent eye, though, and she was astonished when other people took a different view. I was protected from work.

But I only just managed it by the skin of my teeth! Because the time has come when the piled thunderclouds are advancing upon us all. A great healthy storm is brewing, and it's going to blow our society clean of idleness and indifference, clean of prejudice against work and rotting boredom. I'm going to work, but then in twenty years time, in thirty years time, everyone will be working. Every single one of us!

Chebutykin I shan't be working.

Tusenbach You don't count.

[…]

Anfisa (*crossing the drawing-room*) Some strange colonel, my dears! He's taken his coat off, my pets – he's on his way up. Now, Irinushka, you be nice and polite to him … (*Going out*) It's past lunchtime already, too … Oh my lord …

Tusenbach Vershinin, presumably.

Enter Vershinin

Lieutenant-Colonel Vershinin!

Vershinin (*to Masha and Irina*) Allow me to introduce myself – Vershinin. So very glad to be with you at last. But how you've changed! Dear me!

Irina Do sit down. This is a great pleasure for us.

Vershinin (*gaily*) I'm so glad! I'm so glad! But there are three of you, aren't there – three sisters? I remember there being three girls. Your faces I don't recall, but the fact that your father, Colonel Prozorov, had three little girls – that I recall perfectly – indeed I saw it for myself. How time flies! Ah me, how time flies!

Tusenbach The colonel is from Moscow.

Irina From Moscow? You're from Moscow?

Vershinin I am indeed. Your late father was a battery commander there; I was in the same brigade. (*To Masha*) Now your face I believe I do just remember.

Fig. 6.4 *"This is a good healthy Russian climate. The forest, the river…it's birch country…I love it above all trees. It's a fine place to live." Vershinin's enthusiasm for life in the backwoods is reflected in this 1883 painting by Ivan Shishkin*

Masha I don't remember you, though!

Irina Olya! Olya! (*Calls into the main room*) Olya, come here!

Olga comes out of the main room into the drawing-room.

Colonel Vershinin turns out to be from Moscow.

Vershinin So you're Olga, you're the eldest … You're Maria … And you're Irina, you're the youngest …

Olga You're from Moscow?

Vershinin I am. I was at university in Moscow and I began my service career in Moscow. I served there for a long time, until finally I was given a battery here, and transferred, as you see. I don't really remember you – all I remember is that you were three sisters. You father has stayed in my memory very clearly. I sit here and close my eyes and I see him as if he were standing in front of me. I used to come to your house in Moscow …

Olga I thought I remembered them all, and now suddenly …

Irina You're from Moscow … It's like a bolt from the blue!

Olga We're moving there, you see.

Irina We think we shall actually be there by the autumn. It's our home town – we were born there … in Old Basmannaya Street …

She and Olga both laugh with delight.

[…]

Olga Now I've placed you, I remember you.

Vershinin I knew your mother.

Chebutykin A good woman she was, God rest her soul.

Irina Mama's buried in Moscow.

Olga In the Novo-Devichi …

Masha Can you imagine, I'm already beginning to forget her face. It will be the same with us – we shan't be remembered, either. We shall be forgotten.

Vershinin Yes. We shall be forgotten. Such is indeed our fate – there's nothing we can do about it. What we find serious, significant, highly important – the time will come when it's all forgotten, or when it all seems quite unimportant after all.

Pause.

And this is interesting: we can't possible know now what's eventually going to be considered elevated and important, and what people are going to think pathetic and ridiculous. The discoveries made by Copernicus – or Columbus, let's say, didn't they seem uncalled-for and absurd at first? While some empty nonsense written by a crank looked like the truth? And it may be that our present way of life, with which we feel so much at home, will in time seem odd, uncomfortable, foolish, not as clean as it should be – perhaps even wicked.

Tusenbach Who knows? Perhaps, on the other hand, our way of life will be thought elevated and remembered with respect. There's no torture now, no executions or invasions; and yet, at the same time, there's so much suffering.

Solyony (*in a little voice*) Cheep, cheep, cheep … If there's one thing the baron loves it's a nice bit of philosophising.

Tusenbach Will you please leave me alone …? (*Sits elsewhere.*) It's becoming tedious.

Extracts from Three Sisters, *Methuen 2000, pp4–6 and 9–13*

Further reading

Other 19th-century texts in translation include:

- *The Government Inspector* by Nikolai Gogol (1836)
- *Crime and Punishment* by Feodor Dostoevsky (1866)
- *Anna Karenin* by Leo Tolstoy (1875)
- *An Enemy of the People* by Henrik Ibsen (1882)
- *Miss Julie* by August Strindberg (1888).

Questions

AO1: Developing an informed response to the text

- What are the thoughts and feelings of the characters Chekhov presents here?
- What are your personal impressions of these characters? How do you respond to them?

AO2: Understanding how structure, form and language shape meaning

- Explore the dramatic effects Chekhov creates here. You may find it useful to look at the ways in which the characters interact and the different lengths of their lines.
- What do you find interesting about the language Chekhov uses here?
- How does Chekhov make use of specifically Russian details in these extracts?

AO3: Exploring connections, comparisons and the interpretations of other readers

- Why do you think Chekhov's plays have remained so popular throughout the 20th century?
- Some critics claim that Chekhov's dramatic techniques are 'anti-naturalist'. To what extent do the extracts support this view?
- What do you think are the differences between Chekhov's drama and the contemporary English plays featured in this chapter?

AO4: Understanding the significance and influence of contexts

- What does this extract tell us about life in 19th-century Russia?
- Within a decade of the first English performance of Chekhov, the society he presented was destroyed by the Russian Revolution. Can you find any evidence here that Chekhov anticipated this imminent social upheaval?

A screenplay: *The French Lieutenant's Woman*

The shadows cast by the flickering gaslight along smoke-blackened walls, the sound of horses' hooves and carriage wheels on the cobbled streets, the swirling fog drifting in from the river … Our 21st-century impressions of the Victorian era often derive from the ways it has been presented in the cinema or on television. However, it is not just the opportunity to create atmospheric effects that draws film-makers and television producers to the Victorians; the eventful storylines of Dickens, the Brontës and Hardy make their novels popular choices for screen adaptation. Dickens' *Oliver Twist* (1837) provides a good example of the Victorian novel's enduring popularity with film directors: David Lean's evocative monochrome version was made in 1948; Carol Reed's all-singing, all-dancing musical *Oliver!* followed twenty years later; while Roman Polanski revisited the text in his 2005 film.

Perhaps the most literary of these Victorian cinematic adaptations is the film of John Fowles' 1969 novel *The French Lieutenant's Woman*. The film version, directed by Karel Reisz in 1981, features a screenplay by the playwright Harold Pinter. In Chapter 13 of the novel, John Fowles admits to the reader that 'This story I am telling is all imagination. These characters I create never existed outside my own mind.' Fowles presents himself as a modern writer who, aware of the fashionable literary theories of the French structuralists, is unable to become the omniscient author of a traditional Victorian novel because 'I live in the age of Alain Robbe-Grillet and Roland Barthes'. In his screenplay, Pinter similarly reminds the audience that what we are seeing is a construct, not reality: the film's first image shows us the actress who plays Sarah Woodruff checking her costume and make-up before she steps into the role of the heroine. Pinter introduces a second narrative

Fig. 6.5 *"There is a world of difference between what may be accepted in London and what is proper here." Meryl Streep and Jeremy Irons as Anna and Mike playing the roles of Sarah Woodruff and Charles Smithson*

into the screenplay, showing the lives of the actors who portray Fowles' characters: the on-set love affair between Anna and Mike runs parallel to the Victorian love affair of Sarah and Charles. This film-within-a-film is a subtle reminder of the structuralist techniques used in Fowles' novel and also enables Pinter to preserve the alternative endings of the original text.

Mike and Anna feature in the first of these two extracts from Pinter's screenplay. The second extract shows Sarah Woodruff, accompanying Mrs Poulteney on a visit to the home of Mrs Tranter, where they take tea with Mrs Tranter's niece Ernestina and her fiancé Charles Smithson.

Int. Mike's Hotel Room. Lyme Day. Present.

Anna, with glasses on, reading a book. Mike reading the sports page of a newspaper. She looks up.

Anna Wow!

Mike What?

Anna (*referring to the book*) Listen to this.
'In 1857 *The Lancet* estimated that there were eighty thousand prostitutes in the County of London. Out of every sixty houses one was a brothel.'

Mike Mmm.

Pause

Anna (*reading*) 'We reach the surprising conclusion that at a time when the male population of London of all ages was one and a quarter million, the prostitutes were receiving clients at a rate of two million per week.'

Mike Two million!

Anna You know when I say – in the graveyard scene – about going to London? Wait.

She picks up her script of The French Lieutenant's Woman, flips the pages, finds the page. She reads aloud:
'If I went to London I know what I should become. I should become what some already call me in Lyme.'

Mike Yes?

Anna Well, that's what she's really faced with.

(*She picks up the book*)
This man says that hundreds of the prostitutes were nice girls like governesses who had lost their jobs. See what I mean? You offend your boss, you lose your job. That's it! You're on the streets. I mean, it's real.

Mike had picked up a calculator and starts tapping out figures.

Mike The male population was a million and a quarter but the prostitutes had two million clients a week?

Anna Yes. That's what he says.

Mike Allow a third off for boys and old men. That means that outside marriage – a Victorian gentleman had about two point four fucks a week.

She looks at him.

[…]

Mrs Tranter's House. Garden Room. Day.

Mrs Tranter, Mrs Poulteney, Sarah, Ernestina and Charles, sitting.

Mrs Tranter Miss Woodruff, it is a pleasure to meet you. Are you liking Lyme?

Charles looks at Sarah.

Sarah Thank you ma'm. Yes.

Mrs Tranter Were you born far from Lyme?

Sarah In Dorchester ma'm. It is not very far.

A knock on the door. Mary and the Undermaid enter with the tea.

Mrs Tranter Ah, tea! Thank you, Mary.

Mrs Poulteney glares at Mary. Mary ignores her. The maids set the tea.

Mrs Poulteney (*to Ernestina*) How long will you remain in Lyme, Miss Freeman?

Ernestina Oh, for the summer. I must say, Mrs Poulteney, you look exceedingly well.

Mrs Poulteney At my age, Miss Freeman, spiritual health is all that counts.

Ernestina Then I have no fears for you.

Mrs Poulteney With gross disorders on the streets it becomes ever more necessary to protect the sacredness of one's beliefs.

Charles Gross disorders on the streets, Mrs Poulteney?

Mrs Poulteney Certainly, Mr Smithson. Even a disciple of Darwin, such as I understand you to be, could not fail to notice the rise of the animal about us. It no doubt pleases you, since it would accord with your view that we are all monkeys.

Charles I must look more closely into it, Mrs Poulteney, the next time I find myself on a street.

Mary and the Undermaid leave the room. Mrs Tranter begins to pour tea.

She passes a cup to Ernestina.

Sarah (*to Mrs Tranter*) Please allow me to help you, Mrs Tranter.

Mrs Tranter Thank you.

Ernestina gives cup to Mrs Poulteney. Sarah gives cup to Charles.

Mrs Poulteney Your maid, for example. I have been informed that she was seen only this morning talking with a person. A young person.

Charles Then it was no doubt Sam. My servant.

Ernestina gives plate and napkin to Mrs Poulteney. Sarah gives plate and napkin to Charles.

Her hand opens the napkin slightly. He looks down.

Inside the napkin is the corner of an envelope.

Close-Up. Charles.

He looks up quickly.

Int. The Room.

Ernestina Yes, I must say, Charles, your servant spends an inordinate amount of his time talking to Mary.

Charles What is the harm in that?

Ernestina There is a world of difference between what may be accepted in London and what is proper here.

Charles But I do not understand what crime Mary and Sam, by talking, appear to commit.

Mrs Poulteney Your future wife is a better judge than you are of these things, Mr Smithson. I know the girl in question, I had to dismiss her. If you were older you would know that one cannot be too strict in such matters.

Charles I bow to your far greater experience, madam.

The Room.

They all sip tea in silence.

Extracts from Collected Screenplays 3 *by Harold Pinter, Faber 2000, pp22–7 and 45–8*

■ **Further reading**

Other moving-image representations of Victorian literature include:

- *Great Expectations* (David Lean, 1946)
- *Hobson's Choice* (David Lean, 1954)
- *Far from the Madding Crowd* (John Schlesinger, 1967)
- *Tess* (Roman Polanski, 1979)
- *Possession* (Neil LaBute, 2002)
- *The Importance of Being Earnest* (Oliver Parker, 2002).

The Assessment Objectives and the link to keywords in the exam question

You can see how all four Assessment Objectives are assessed in this question:

AO1 is always tested in all questions.

AO2 is tested in the first bullet point with the words 'the ways the writer expresses them', and in the second bullet point in the word 'style'.

AO3 is tested in the first bullet point where you are asked to 'consider the writer's thoughts and feelings', and in the second bullet point where the examiner asks you to 'compare the extract with your wider reading'.

AO4 is tested in the second bullet point where the examiner asks 'how typical' this extract is of Victorian literature.

Remember that the keywords you will need to focus on as you attempt the context question are:

■ context
■ thoughts and feelings
■ compare
■ how typical
■ subject matter
■ style.

Practising the skills

You are now going to practise your skills by looking at five extracts from Victorian non-fiction. You will need to:

■ read each extract carefully
■ look for evidence of the writer's thoughts and feelings
■ analyse the writer's choices of form, structure and language, and how they shape meaning
■ make connections between the extract and your wider reading
■ assess the typicality of attitude and style of the extract.

As you make connections between the extract and your wider reading, you should try to think of at least one prose, one drama and one poetry text or extract that you have read.

If you are working in a group with other students, you will find it useful to share and compare your ideas.

A letter: William Wordsworth to General Charles Pasley

Although William Wordsworth (1770–1850) is best known as the foremost English poet of the Romantic movement, it should be remembered that he also lived through the first 13 years of the Victorian era. Despite the revolutionary sentiments expressed in the great poetry of his youth, Wordsworth became a figurehead of the Establishment in later life and was appointed Poet Laureate to Queen Victoria in 1843.

Wordsworth wrote the letter below on 15 October 1844: General Charles Pasley was a family friend who was also the government's Inspector General of Railways. Although Wordsworth had celebrated the railways as a symbol of progress in his 1833 sonnet 'Steamboats, Viaducts, and Railways', his attitude towards them changed as the railway companies began to plan lines through the Lake District: the day after he wrote this letter, his protest poem 'On the Projected Kendal and Windermere Railway' appeared in the *Morning Post* newspaper.

… all the old resident Gentlemen and Proprietors of the neighbourhood are greatly annoyed, with scarcely an exception, by the project of a Railway from Kendal to the head of Windermere. The shares are already subscribed for and at a premium, which will not surprise you who are better, probably, than anyone else, acquainted with the excesses to which the Railway Mania drives people on the present superabundances of Capital. Excuse my writing to you upon this occasion which I do beg that when it comes before you, as probably it will, you would give it more attention than its apparent importance may call for. The traffic will be found quite contemptible, the staple of this country is its beauty and that will be destroyed by such a nuisance being carried through these narrow vales, at present nothing is publicly said of its being carried farther than within a mile of Ambleside, but that is all nonsense. Attempts will assuredly be made and at no distant Period, to carry it on to Keswick, to Maryport, notwithstanding the high ground that parts Westmorland from Cumberland.

© National Gallery, London

Fig. 7.1 *"The Staple of the country is its beauty and that will be destroyed." Unlike Wordsworth, the painter Turner was able to absorb the railway into his Romantic vision of the landscape. This is 'Rain, Speed and Steam – The Great Western Railway' (1844)*

Questions

AO1: Developing an informed response to the text

- What are Wordsworth's thoughts and feelings about 'the Railway Mania'?

- What are Wordsworth's main objections to the proposed railway line?

AO2: Understanding how structure, form and language shape meaning

- How does Wordsworth structure and develop his argument in this letter?

- Consider the ways that Wordsworth's choices of language shape his meaning here.

- What impressions do you form of Wordsworth's friendship with Pasley from this letter?

AO3: Exploring connections, comparisons and the interpretations of other readers

- What connections can you make between Wordsworth's thoughts and feelings here and those you have discovered elsewhere in your wider reading?

- How does this letter compare with other Victorian letters that you have read? In making your comparisons, you should consider both subject matter and style.

- Compare Wordsworth's views here with those expressed by John Ruskin in the letter that appears in the sample exam paper (see Chapter 8).

AO4: Understanding the significance and influence of contexts

- Are the views Wordsworth expresses here typical of 19th-century attitudes to railway construction?

- Wordsworth's greatest fame was as a nature poet: what evidence of his attitudes to nature can you find in this letter?

Further reading

- *Steamboats, Viaducts, and Railways* and *On the Projected Kendal and Windermere Railway* by William Wordsworth.

- *Wordsworth: A Life in Letters* (ed. Barker, 2002).

- *Locksley Hall* by Alfred Lord Tennyson (1842): a remarkably futuristic poem, in which railway tracks are used as a symbol of universal progress ('Let the great world spin for ever down the ringing grooves of change.') as Tennyson predicts the invention of fighter aircraft ('the nations' airy navies grappling in the central blue') and prophesies ultimate world peace ('Till the war-drum throbb'd no longer, and the battle-flags were furl'd / In the Parliament of man, the Federation of the world.').

- *The Signal-Man* by Charles Dickens (1866): the railwayman of the title is haunted by a sinister apparition at the tunnel mouth beyond his signal-box.

- *Middlemarch* by George Eliot (1871), particularly Chapter 56, in which a group of railway surveyors are threatened by pitchfork-wielding yokels.

- *La Bête humaine* by Emile Zola (1890): the French railway system provides the symbolic setting for this dark novel of twisted passions.

An autobiography: Journey out of Essex

John Clare (1793–1864) was the publishing sensation of 1820: marketed as 'The Northamptonshire Peasant Poet', he became a familiar figure on the London literary scene and his first collection, *Poems Descriptive of Rural Life and Scenery*, sold out three editions within a year. Unfortunately, when Clare's subsequent volumes failed to sell, he became increasingly depressed and disturbed: in 1837, he was admitted to a private hospital for the insane at High Beach, Epping. Four years later, Clare escaped from High Beach and walked the 90 miles back to Northborough, Northamptonshire in four days. Clare was in a deluded state at the time, believing that he was married to two women: his real wife, Patty, mother of his six children; and his long-dead childhood sweetheart, Mary Joyce. Clare wrote his account of the long walk north from Essex within days of returning to his family: the extract below presents the last stage of his journey. Clare did not remain at home for long: five months later he was committed to the Northampton General Lunatic Asylum and remained there for the rest of his life.

Fig. 7.2 *'Before The Fall'. At the height of his fame in 1820, John Clare had his portrait painted by the fashionable society artist, William Hilton*

Further reading

■ *John Clare by Himself* (ed. Robinson and Powell, 1996): Clare's collected autobiographical writings.

■ *John Clare: A Biography* by Jonathan Bate (2003).

■ *Edge of the Orison* by Iain Sinclair (2005): Clare's journey retraced by a 21st-century psychogeographer.

■ *Kilvert's Diary 1870–1879*: a vicar's view of mid-Victorian rural life.

[July 23rd 1841] before I got to Peterborough a man and woman passed me in a cart and on hailing me as they passed I found they were neighbours from Helpstone where I used to live – I told them I was knocked up which they could easily see and that I had neither eat nor drank anything since I left Essex when I told my story they clubbed together and threw me fivepence out of the cart I picked it up and called at a small public house near the bridge where I had two half pints of ale and twopenn'oth of bread and cheese when I had done I started quite refreshed only my feet was more crippled than ever and I could scarcely make a walk of it over the stones and being half ashamed to sit down in the street I forced to keep on the move and got through Peterborough better than I expected when I got on the high road I rested on the stone heaps as I passed till I was able to go on afresh and bye and bye I passed Walton and soon reached Werrington and was making for the Beehive as fast as I could when a cart met me with a man and a woman and a boy in it when nearing me the woman jumped out and caught fast hold of my hands and wished me to get into the cart but I refused and thought her either drunk or mad but when I was told it was my second wife Patty I got in and was soon at Northborough but Mary was not there neither could I get any information about her further than the old story of her being dead six years ago which might be taken from a bran new old Newspaper printed a dozen years ago but I took no notice of the blarney having seen her myself about a twelvemonth ago alive and well and as young as ever – so here I am homeless at home and half gratified to feel that I can be happy anywhere…

[July 24th 1841] Returned home out of Essex and found no Mary – her and her family are as nothing to me now though she herself was once the dearest of all – 'and how can I forget'.

Questions

AO1: Developing an informed response to the text

- What are the main events Clare describes on the last stage of his journey?
- What are your impressions of the people and places Clare describes in this passage?
- How does this passage reveal Clare's disturbed state of mind to the reader?

AO2: Understanding how structure, form and language shape meaning

- What do you notice about the ways in which Clare expresses his thoughts and feelings here?
- Clare had little formal education and avoided using punctuation marks, calling them 'the awkward squad'. What effects does this have on his prose style?
- Explore the ways that Clare's choices of language shape his meaning here.

- Consider the effect of Clare's claim that he 'thought her either drunk or mad'.

AO3: Exploring connections, comparisons and the interpretations of other readers

- What connections can you make between Clare's thoughts and feelings here and those you have discovered elsewhere in your wider reading?
- How does Clare's autobiographical writing compare with other 19th-century autobiographies that you have read? In making your comparisons, you should consider both subject matter and style.

AO4: Understanding the significance and influence of contexts

- Do you think Clare's *Journey out of Essex* is typical of Victorian literature?
- What does this passage show us about rural life in the 19th century?

A biography: The Life of Charlotte Brontë

Elizabeth Gaskell (1810–65) was a successful and controversial Victorian novelist: her best-seller *Mary Barton* (1848) was criticised for its hostile presentation of exploitative Manchester factory owners, while *Ruth* (1853) offers a sympathetic portrait of an unmarried mother (an almost unmentionable subject for some mid-19th-century readers). Gaskell was a close friend of the novelist Charlotte Brontë (1816–55) and her *Life of Charlotte Brontë* (1857) was the first major Brontë biography. Like Gaskell's novels, *The Life of Charlotte Brontë* met with a mixed reception: she was forced to revise several passages of the book after receiving complaints and threats of legal action from some of the people she had written about. Although later biographers, such as Juliet Barker, have questioned some of the claims Gaskell made (her treatment of Charlotte's father seems to be particularly harsh: the Reverend Patrick Brontë is presented as an insensitive and unsympathetic parent), *The Life of Charlotte Brontë* remains an important example of Victorian literary biography. It was certainly a very influential book, providing an important stimulus to the incipient cult of the Brontë family – a cult which has today turned the Brontës' Haworth home into a literary shrine second only to Stratford-upon-Avon.

In this extract, Gaskell describes the conditions at Cowan Bridge School, which Charlotte Brontë attended in 1824, along with her three sisters.

> …the cook…was careless, dirty, and wasteful. To some children oatmeal porridge is distasteful, and consequently unwholesome, even when properly made; at Cowan Bridge School it was often sent up, not merely burnt, but with offensive fragments of other substances discoverable in it. The beef, that should have been carefully salted before it was dressed, had often become tainted from neglect; and girls who were school-fellows of the Brontës, during the reign of the cook of whom I am speaking, tell me that the house seemed to be pervaded, morning, noon, and night, by the odour of rancid fat that steamed out of the oven in which much of their food was prepared. There was the same carelessness in making the puddings; one of

Fig. 7.3 *'The weird sisters'.*
Anne, Emily and Charlotte, painted by
their brother Branwell in 1834

those ordered was rice boiled in water, and eaten with a sauce of treacle and sugar; but it was often uneatable, because the water had been taken out of the rain tub, and was strongly impregnated with the dust lodging on the roof, whence it had trickled down into the old wooden cask, which also added its own flavour to that of the original rain water. The milk, too, was often 'bingy', to use a country expression for a kind of taint that is far worse than sourness, and suggests the idea that it is caused by want of cleanliness about the milk pans, rather than by the heat of the weather. On Saturdays a kind of pie, or mixture of potatoes and meat, was served up, which was made of all the fragments accumulated during the week. Scraps of meat from a dirty and disorderly larder could never be very appetizing; and I believe that this dinner was more loathed than any in the early days of Cowan Bridge School. One may fancy how repulsive such fare would be to children whose appetites were small, and who had been accustomed to food, far simpler perhaps, but prepared with a delicate cleanliness that made it both tempting and wholesome. At many a meal the little Brontës went without food, although craving with hunger.

■ Questions

AO1: Developing an informed response to the text

■ What are the main features of Cowan Bridge School described by Gaskell in this extract?

■ What are Gaskell's feelings about the conditions at the school?

AO2: Understanding how structure, form and language shape meaning

■ What do you notice about the ways in which Gaskell expresses her thoughts and feelings here?

■ Consider the effects created by Gaskell's language, especially her choice of adjectives.

■ How does Gaskell create sympathy for the Brontës in this extract?

AO3: Exploring connections, comparisons and the interpretations of other readers

■ How does Gaskell's writing compare with other Victorian biographies that you have read? In making your comparisons, you should consider both subject matter and style.

■ Compare Gaskell's presentation of Cowan Bridge with other Victorian schools you have read about.

■ Compare this extract with the description of Lowood in Chapter 5 of *Jane Eyre*.

AO4: Understanding the significance and influence of contexts

■ Are Gaskell's attitudes to school conditions typical of 19th-century writers?

■ What does this extract tell you about the ways that Victorian schools treated their pupils?

■ Do you think there were any complaints about what Gaskell wrote in this passage? If so, who might have complained and why?

■ Further reading

■ *Jane Eyre* by Charlotte Brontë (1847), particularly Chapter 5 which contains significant parallels to the above passage from Gaskell's biography.

■ *The Brontës* by Juliet Barker (1994).

■ *The Brontës: A Life in Letters* (ed. Barker, 1997).

■ *Hard Times* (1854) by Charles Dickens, particularly Chapters 1 and 2 which describe Coketown school.

■ *Eminent Victorians* by Lytton Strachey (1918): this provocative and controversial biography sets the tone for much 20th-century writing about Victorian lives.

A history text in translation: The Condition of the Working Class in England

Friedrich Engels (1820–95), the son of a German manufacturer, lived in Manchester for two years during the 1840s while he supervised the Lancashire branch of the family business. He witnessed the city's industrial transformation at first hand and, shocked by the conditions in which working people were forced to live, he recorded his observations in *The Condition of the Working Class in England* (1845). The book was originally written in German, but Engels translated it into English himself for the American edition of 1886. Perhaps unsurprisingly, Engels' scathing exposé of British poverty and deprivation was not published in this country until 1892. Engels became an increasingly active political champion of the proletariat: in 1848, with Karl Marx, he wrote *The Communist Manifesto*.

In this extract from *The Condition of the Working Class in England*, Engels describes the Ducie Bridge area of Manchester and the slums along the banks of the river Irk.

> Everywhere heaps of debris, refuse, and offal: standing pools for gutters, and a stench which alone would make it impossible for a human being in any degree civilized to live in such a district … Immediately under the railway bridge there stands a court, the filth and horrors of which surpass the others by far … Passing along a rough bank, among stakes and washing lines, one penetrates into this chaos of small one-storeyed, one-roomed hovels, in most of which there is no artificial floor; kitchen, living and sleeping-room all in one. In such a hole, scarcely five feet long by six broad, I found two beds – and such bedsteads and beds! – which, with a staircase and chimney-place, entirely filled the room … Everywhere before the doors refuse and offal; that any sort of pavement lay underneath could not be seen but only felt, here and there, with the feet. This whole collection of cattle-sheds for human beings was surrounded on

Fig. 7.4 *Although Eyre Crowe was praised for the realism of his industrial paintings, 'The Dinner Hour, Wigan' (1875) depicts a more sanitised version of Victorian Lancashire than the one reported by Engels*

Further reading

■ *Mary Barton* by Elizabeth Gaskell (1848): this novel is subtitled *A Tale of Manchester Life*.

■ *Past and Present* by Thomas Carlyle (1843): Engels wrote that Carlyle was the only British social commentator fully to understand the plight of the working class. The complexity and breadth of Carlyle's thoughts can make his writing something of a challenge to 21st-century readers, but the handy Penguin anthology, *Selected Writings of Thomas Carlyle*, breaks his massive output down into more manageable chunks.

■ *London Labour and the London Poor* by Henry Mayhew (1849): Mayhew scrutinises living and working conditions in the capital, using the same documentary methods as Engels in Manchester.

■ *A Child of the Jago* by Arthur Morrison (1896): an autobiographical account of life in London's slums.

■ *The Communist Manifesto* by Karl Marx and Friedrich Engels (1848).

■ *The Cry of the Children* by Elizabeth Barrett Browning (1843): Browning's poem about Victorian factory conditions was part of a campaign for legal restrictions on the use of child labour.

two sides by houses and a factory, and on the third by the river, and besides the narrow stair up the bank, a narrow doorway alone led out into another almost equally ill-built, ill-kept labyrinth of dwellings.

Enough! The whole side of the Irk is built in this way, a planless, knotted chaos of houses, more or less on the verge of uninhabitableness, whose unclean interiors fully correspond with their filthy external surroundings. And how could the people be clean with no proper opportunity for satisfying the most natural and ordinary wants? Privies are so rare here that they are either filled up every day, or are too remote for most of the inhabitants to use. How can people wash when they have only the dirty Irk water at hand, while pumps and water pipes can be found in decent parts of the city alone?

Questions

AO1: Developing an informed response to the text

- What are the main features of the district Engels describes in this extract?
- What are Engels' feelings about what he witnesses here?

AO2: Understanding how structure, form and language shape meaning

- Which words in Engels' description do you find particularly powerful or effective?
- What effects does Engels create by using exclamations and rhetorical questions in this extract?
- Look carefully at how Engels develops his ideas and his line of argument. What do you find interesting about the ways he structures this passage?

AO3: Exploring connections, comparisons and the interpretations of other readers

- What connections can you make between Engels' thoughts and feelings here and those you have discovered elsewhere in your wider reading?

- How does Engels' writing compare with other Victorian history texts that you have read? In making your comparisons, you should consider both subject matter and style.
- Using the extracts in Chapter 5, compare Engels' presentation of Victorian poverty in Manchester with Herman Melville's presentation of conditions in 19th-century Liverpool.

AO4: Understanding the significance and influence of contexts

- Do you think the political views Engels expresses here are typical of 19th-century writing?
- What does this passage tell us about the lives of the working classes in the Victorian era?
- Why do you think this book was not published in Britain until nearly fifty years after it was written?

Cultural commentary: Modern Painters

John Ruskin (1819–1900) was one of the most important cultural commentators of the 19th century. As an art critic, he championed the causes of radical new painters such as J.M.W. Turner and the Pre-Raphaelites, but he is perhaps best known today for the two controversial court cases which seriously affected his reputation. In 1854 his marriage to Euphemia Gray was annulled on the grounds of non-consummation, while in 1878 he was sued for libel by James McNeill Whistler after he had accused the American artist of 'flinging a pot of paint in the public's face'. To us, this seems a surprising response: the painting to which Ruskin objected, 'The Falling Rocket', is an impressionistic view of London at night, featuring the sort of artistic effects pioneered by Turner 50 years earlier. Although Ruskin lost the case, the judge obviously thought that he had a point: Whistler was awarded damages of one farthing (the smallest British coin then in circulation, worth a quarter of a penny!).

The extract below is taken from *Modern Painters I* (1843). Ruskin is describing Turner's 1840 painting 'Slavers throwing overboard the dead and dying – Typhoon coming on'.

I think the noblest sea that Turner has ever painted … is that of the Slave Ship. It is a sunset on the Atlantic, after prolonged storm; but the storm is partially lulled, and the torn and streaming rain-clouds are moving in scarlet lines to lose themselves in the hollow of the night. The whole surface of the sea included in the picture is divided into two ridges of enormous swell, not high, nor local, but a low broad heaving of the whole ocean, like the lifting of its bosom by deep-drawn breath after the torture of the storm. Between these two ridges the fire of sunset falls along the trough of the sea, dyeing it with an awful but glorious light, the intense and lurid splendour which burns like gold, and bathes like blood … Purple and blue, the lurid shadows of the hollow breakers are cast upon the mist of night, which gathers cold and low, advancing like the shadow of death upon the guilty* ship as it labours amid the lightning of the sea, its thin masts written upon the sky in lines of blood, girded with condemnation in that fearful hue which signs the sky with horror, and mixes its flaming flood with the sunlight, and, cast far along the desolate heave of the sepulchral waves, incarnadines the multitudinous sea.

_____

* She is a slaver, throwing her slaves overboard. The near sea is encumbered with corpses.

Fig. 7.5 *"Two hundred guineas for flinging a pot of paint in the public's face". Ruskin's later art criticism became increasingly hysterical: his attack on Whistler's 'Nocturne in Black and Gold: The Falling Rocket' (1875) led to a court case which damaged the reputations of both men*

Questions

AO1: Developing an informed response to the text

■ What are the main features of the picture, according to Ruskin's description?

■ What are Ruskin's thoughts and feelings about this painting and about its subject matter?

AO2: Understanding how structure, form and language shape meaning

■ What do you notice about the ways in which Ruskin expresses his thoughts and feelings here?

■ Consider the effects created by Ruskin's vocabulary in this extract, especially his use of colours.

■ Explore the ways in which Ruskin's repeated references to blood help to shape his meaning in this extract.

AO3: Exploring connections, comparisons and the interpretations of other readers

■ What connections can you make between Ruskin's thoughts and feelings here and those you have discovered elsewhere in your wider reading?

■ In his literary criticism, Ruskin coined the phrase 'the pathetic fallacy' to describe the way that writers present the mood of nature as sometimes in sympathy with human events. Do you think that Ruskin is employing the pathetic fallacy himself in this passage?

■ The Ruskin biographer John Batchelor claims that this passage shows 'Ruskin's response to this painting is aesthetic to the exclusion of almost all else'. To what extent do you agree with this view?

AO4: Understanding the significance and influence of contexts

■ Do you think Ruskin's writing is typical of Victorian cultural commentary?

■ What does this passage tell you about 19th-century attitudes to art?

Conclusion: a specimen paper

Aims of the chapter:

- Reviews the skills and knowledge gained through your AS English Literature course and study of this book.

- Introduces a specimen exam paper where you can practise your skills and identify where you might need to improve them.

- Looks at ways of approaching the exam paper.

- Explains how you will be assessed.

Link

In Chapter 2 we explored the kinds of questions that will be asked on your set poetry text; one of the suggested activities was to make up your own questions addressing the three relevant Assessment Objectives.

Link

In Chapter 7 we looked in detail at the kinds of extracts you could expect to find in the context question on the exam paper, ending the chapter with an example of a specimen context question.

Introduction

By the time you have worked through this book and are approaching your AS English Literature exam, you will need to start thinking about how you are going to:

- **use the knowledge** you have gathered, through your study of the set texts and your wider reading of Victorian literature, in the exam;

- **demonstrate the skills** you have been practising through the **activities**.

Your coursework essays should now be written, but remember that your knowledge of your two chosen coursework texts – the play and the novel – is relevant to the context question on the exam paper. In addition, you should have a Reading Log of all the wider reading you have done in prose, poetry and drama of the Victorian era; this log will either be in the form of written notes or a file on the computer. These notes should form the basis of your revision for the exam paper.

The specimen paper

The best way to prepare for the real exam is to **practise answering questions** of the type that you will be asked. You can, of course, **make up your own questions** – alone, or in a group, and with the help of your teacher. If you do this, you need to follow the models provided in this book.

What follows now is a complete specimen paper. How you use it is for you to decide. You and your teacher may wish to use it as a 'mock' exam, sitting down and writing for two hours under examination conditions. Or you may wish to look at the questions alone or in a group, brainstorming what materials you might use, how you might structure your answers and then comparing notes, before you write the relevant essays.

Read through the following paper carefully and closely.

AQA Examination-style questions

Unit 1 Texts in Context

Time allowed 2 hours

Candidates must answer **two** questions:

- the compulsory question in **Section A**
- one question in **Section B**.

OPTION A: VICTORIAN LITERATURE
SECTION A: CONTEXTUAL LINKING

Answer Question 1.

1   Read the following extract carefully. It is taken from *Fors Clavigera*, a series of open letters to the public written by John Ruskin. In this letter Ruskin expresses his views on the Midland Railway's construction of a line through Monsal Dale, Derbyshire in 1863.

In your answer you should:

- consider the writer's thoughts and feelings about aspects of Victorian life and the ways in which he expresses them
- compare this extract to your wider reading, saying how typical you think it is of Victorian literature. You should consider both subject matter and style.

(45 marks)

There was a rocky valley between Buxton and Bakewell, once upon a time, divine as the Vale of Tempe; you might have seen the Gods there morning and evening – Apollo and all the sweet Muses of the Light – walking in fair procession on the lawns of it, and to and fro among the pinnacles of its crags. You cared neither for Gods nor grass, but for cash (which you did not know the way to get); you thought you could get it by what the Times calls 'Railroad Enterprise.' You Enterprised a Railroad through the valley – you blasted its rocks away, heaped thousands of tons of shale into its lovely stream. The valley is gone, and the Gods with it; and now, every fool in Buxton can be at Bakewell in half-an-hour, and every fool in Bakewell at Buxton; which you think a lucrative process of exchange – you Fools Everywhere.

Fig. 8.1 *'You cared neither for Gods nor grass, but for cash'. The London and Birmingham Railway cuts its way through the Northamptonshire countryside in this 1837 drawing by J. C. Bourne*